Blogging with WordPress 3 for Beginners
Copyright © 2010 by B.M.Harwani

All rights reserved. No part of this work may be reproduced or transmitted in any form or by any means, electronic or mechanical, including photocopying, recording, or by any information storage or retrieval system, without the prior written permission of the copyright owner.

Trademarked names may appear in this book. Rather than use a trademark symbol with every occurrence of a trademarked name, I use the names only in an editorial fashion and to the benefit of the trademark owner, with no intention of infringement of the trademark.

All brand names and product names used in this book are trademarks, registered trademarks, or trade names of the irrespective holders. The author is not associated with any product or vendor mentioned in this book.

The information in this book is distributed without warranty. Although every precaution has been taken in the preparation of the work, the author shall have no liability to any person or entity with respect to any loss or damage caused or alleged to be caused directly or indirectly by the information contained in this work.

The author makes no representation or warranties with respect to the accuracy or completeness of the information contained in this work and is not responsible for any errors, omissions, or damages arising out of use of this information.

For information on translations, please email *bmharwani@yahoo.com*

Edition: 2010

Dedicated to three Gems of my motherland:

Amitabh Bachchan, a great actor, producer and superstar of Bollywood cinema

Sachin Ramesh Tendulkar (Master Blaster), a great batsmen and player in the history of cricket

Lata Mangeshkar nicknamed the 'nightingale of India', a most well known playback singer

Acknowledgements

I am very thankful to my family—my small world: Anushka (my wife) and my two little darlings, Chirag and Naman, for allowing me to work on the book when I was supposed to spend time with them.

I also thankful to my dear students, who have been good teachers for me, as they make me aware of the basic programming problems they face, enabling me to address that which puzzles them. The endless, interesting student queries has helped me to write books with a practical approach.

About the Author

B. M. Harwani is the managing director of the Computer Education Centre - Microchip Computer Education (MCE), based in Ajmer, India. He graduated with a BE in computer engineering from the University of Pune, and has a 'C' Level master's diploma in computer technology from DOEACC, Government Of India. Involved in teaching field for over 15 years, Mr. Harwani has developed the art of explaining even the most complicated topics in a manner that everybody can easily understand. He has written many successful books, including *Programming & Problem Solving through C* (BPB, 2004), *Learn Tally in Just Three Weeks* (Pragya, 2005), *Data Structures and Algorithms through C* (CBC, 2006), *Master Unix Shell Programming* (CBC, 2006), *Business Systems* (CBC, 2006), *Practical Java Projects* (Shroff, 2007), *Practical Web Services* (Shroff, 2007), *Java for Professionals* (Shroff, 2008), *C++ for Beginners* (Shroff, 2009), *Practical ASP.NET 3.5 Projects* (Shroff, 2009), *Java Server Faces—A Practical Approach for Beginners* (PHI Learning, 2009), *Practical JSF Project using NetBeans* (PHI Learning, 2009), *Foundation Joomla* (Friends of ED, 2009), *Practical EJB Projects* (Shroff, 2009), *Data Structures and Algorithms in C++* (Dreamtech Press, 2010), *Developing Web Applications in PHP and AJAX* (Tata McGraw Hill, 2010), and *jQuery Recipes* (Apress, 2010). He can be contacted at **bmharwani@yahoo.com**.

Organization of the book

The book contains eight chapters. An overview of their contents is as under:

Chapter 1, Introduction: The chapter covers introduction to Blogging, WordPress and its features. Also different ways of installing WordPress are explained step by step. The first things that we get come across on creation of a blog, the Main Navigation Menu and Dashboard are also explained in this chapter

Chapter 2, Posts and Pages: In this chapter, you will learn to create and manage the contents of our website. Posts and pages are the two important ways to create content for a blog, hence both are covered in detail.

Chapter 3, Managing Media, Links and Comments: This chapter explains the working with Media, Links and Comments. Media, i.e. images, audio, video and other files are the important and essential part of content, so the chapter explains how to use Media Library for managing media. Links are the popular means for navigation. In this chapter, you will learn to create a new link category, manage links in the link category and understand links of the Blogroll (a default link category provided by the WordPress). Comments are the responses of the visitors on the posts published on a blog. The chapter covers the process of moderating comments that is, how to delete comments, mark them as spam, edit and approve them.

Chapter 4, Making the Blog Dynamic : In this chapter, you will learn to manage themes, custom menus and widgets. Themes are the best means to make a blog appear attractive and dynamic. The chapter explains how to search, install and activate and deactivate themes. Custom Menus are used at large for developing navigation, i.e., adding links and internal and external URLs to pages. In this chapter, you will learn to create, add and remove links from the custom menus. Widgets are highly used for displaying required information on the sidebars. In this chapter, you will learn the usage of each of these widgets in detail and understand how each widget is configured to display the required information. The chapter also explains the role of the theme editor in editing the selected theme.

Chapter 5, Users and Roles: In this chapter, you will learn to manage user accounts, roles and setting profiles. Users are the persons that visit, access, contribute and administer our blog. In this chapter, you will learn how the users are created, edited and deleted. The roles are the best mechanism to assign privileges to the users of our blog. In this chapter, you will learn different types of pre-defined roles and the rights or permissions attached to each of them. The chapter also explains how a user can enter and set personal information through Profiles.

Chapter 6, Using Plugins: In this chapter, you will learn to extend features of our blog through plugins. The chapter explains how to install, activate, delete, upgrade and edit plugins.

Chapter 7, Tools and Settings: In this chapter, you will be learning about two important menus of WordPress, Tools and Settings. Using these menus, you will be learning to use Press This tool to grab web pages found on the net, import contents from different blogging platforms into a WordPress blog, export contents of a WordPress blog, allow visitors to register on a blog, set Date and Time format, submit posts via email, perform remote publishing, i.e., submit posts from a desktop client, define default sizes for media files, control visibility of our blog, generate search engine friendly URLs through Permalink Settings

Chapter 8, Lots More : This chapter covers several things like, translating a blog into different languages, integrating a blog with Facebook and Twitter, taking Online Backup, generating XML Sitemaps, allowing visitors to subscribe and displaying advertisement for revenue

Table of Contents

1

Introduction

This chapter covers the following:

- Introduction to Blogging
- Introduction to WordPress and its features
- Different ways of installing WordPress
- Main Navigation Menu and Dashboard

Let us begin the chapter by understanding the term blogging.

1.1 Blogging

A blog is a short form of weblog which means an interactive website where an individual can post his/her personal thoughts, events, graphics or video. A blog may contain text, images and links to other blogs and media. The person who creates a blog is known as *blogger* and the procedure of updating a blog is known as *blogging*. The blogs are usually updated daily and the posts published on the blog are by default arranged in chronological order with the most recent post at the top. Visitors of the blogs can view posts and share their views by writing comments.

Blogging can be done on several platforms. Few of such blogging platforms are listed as follows:

- **Blogger**—Blogger is a popular and free blogging service owned by Google. It supports several features such as drag and drop template editing, dynamic updating, geo-tagging for location-based blogging and allows easy publication through editing tools such as Google Docs, Microsoft Word and Windows Live Writer.

- **Tumblr**—Tumblr is the fusion of a fully featured blog and a Twitter feed. This platform is popularly used for short and frequent posts.

- **WordPress**—WordPress is the most widely used open-source blogging platform, which is very easy to install and configure. In just a few minutes, you can see your blog up and running.

- **SquareSpace**—SquareSpace is a commercial blogging platform focused on making good blog design easy for newbies. Since it uses a modular design, creating a new blog is very easy; just by connecting different modules.

- **Posterous**—Blogging in Posterous platform is very easy; just by emailing at post@posterous.com the platform creates a blog YourName.Posterous.com.

- **LiveJournal**—LiveJournal is basically a community collaboration tool that allows us to form networks of friends and blogs online.

- **TypePad**—TypePad provides several easy to use tools to customize colors, fonts and images of the blog. Even a novice can easily submit posts and photos.

- **Movable Type**—Movable Type is a commercial blogging platform. Its administrative user interface is clean and polished and its tag language is very easy to learn.

- **ExpressionEngine**—ExpressionEngine is a flexible and powerful tool that is targeted at more tech-savvy bloggers. It allows us to configure its settings at a very detailed level.

Since, this book is focused on creating blogs through WordPress, let us go ahead and introduce ourselves to the world of WordPress.

1.2 WordPress—An Introduction

WordPress is the most popular blog and content management system used for creating websites for personal, businesses, university departments, etc. It requires PHP and MySQL database and can run on several web servers including Apache and IIS. WordPress provides us a web-based interface that makes the job of maintaining a site very easy. Instead of doing the tedious task of editing or uploading files to the server manually, we can easily and quickly maintain the blog through the user-friendly web based interface.

Note: With WordPress not only can we make blogs that are packed with features but also websites that are lightning fast.

All the things required for developing a website are provided by WordPress. Its core system includes:

- **Posts and Pages**—Posts and Pages are a good means of delivering information. The information of static nature that does not change frequently such as the information delivered via *About Us* or *Contact Us* web pages are displayed through Pages. The information that is of dynamic nature and is focused on updating our visitors is displayed through Posts. Posts are always associated with a date.

- **Media files**—The media files including images, audio, video, PDFs, etc. that are inserted into Posts or Pages are maintained through Media Library in WordPress.

- **Categorized Links**—Links play a major role in implementing navigation on a website. The links whether internal or external are categorized in WordPress into link categories. By default, WordPress comes with a link category called *Blogroll*.

- **Categories and Tags**—In WordPress, the posts can be divided into different categories on the basis of their subject so that visitors can find content related to a particular subject at one place. For example, the posts can be categorized into different categories such as programming, web designing, etc. Also, posts can be described through keywords known as *tags*. The tags help the search engine in locating the post. For example, a post titled, *Implementing AJAX in PHP* may have the tags such as AJAX, PHP, JavaScript and XML.

- **User Roles and Profiles**—WordPress provides a very easy mechanism for creating users, defining their personal information and assigning roles to them. It also includes some pre-defined roles such as *Subscriber, Contributor, Author, Editor* and *Administrator* where each role has different privileges and capabilities to access different components of a website.

- **RSS and ATOM Feeds**—To implement communication of information between different sites, WordPress makes RSS and Atom feeds available for contents of our blog including posts, comments, etc. hence allowing other sites to consume our feeds. Also, we can import the RSS or ATOM feeds from other sites and publish them on our own.

- **Search Engine friendly URLs**—WordPress supports search engine friendly URLs for the published contents also known as Permalinks.

- **AntiSpam plugin**—WordPress comes with an antispam plugin, the *Akismet* plugin that scans comments for spam on submission. These comments if detected as spam are automatically ignored and are not published on our website.

Let us have a quick look at the different features of WordPress.

1.2.1 WordPress Features

WordPress is a popular blogging platform that combines the attributes, features and benefits of a standard website and a blog. A few of its features are as listed as follows:

- **No Cost**—WordPress is an open-source software, i.e., there is no extra cost involved in using it personally or commercially.

- **Standards Compliant**—WordPress adheres to Web Standards and is compatible with all popular browsers.

- **Easy to Use**—The user interface of WordPress is very easy to understand and to work with which makes the job of maintaining the blog quite easy without needing a Web master.

- **Easy to install and upgrade**—WordPress is very easy to install. Also, upgrading the weblog to the latest version of WordPress is very easy, too. In fact, it can be done automatically.

- **Internationalization and Localization**—The weblog can be localized to our choice and translated to any language of our choice.

- **UTC friendly**—WordPress allows us to define our time as an offset *from Universal Coordinated Time (UTC)*, i.e., all the information related to time is stored in the database in the form of GMT values that is a universal standard.

- **Communication of information**—WordPress supports RSS 1.0, RSS 2.0 and ATOM specifications. Every page of our weblog has an associated feed that our readers can subscribe to.

- **Archives**—WordPress not only organizes our posts but also archives our old posts. We can see yearly, monthly, weekly, daily, category-wise or author-wise archives.

- **Searching**—WordPress has a built-in search tool that allows visitors to search for the desired posts or pages in our blog.

- **Feedback**—WordPress is very helpful in providing information to our visitors and getting feedback from them in the form of comments. That is, visitors can give their views in the form of comments to different posts published on our blog.

- **Notification**—WordPress informs each time there is a new comment or a post submitted on our blog by sending an email. Also, a notification is sent when some other blog links to any of posts in our blog.

- **Extendibility**—Features of our WordPress blog can be extended by installing and activating different plugins that are freely available. Through plugins, we can easily add features such as site map, polls, shopping cart, Facebook and Twitter integration, advertising, etc. to our blog.

- **Themes Support**—WordPress uses themes to change the look-and-feel of our blog. We can make our blog attractive just by applying themes.

- **Community Support**—There is a large WordPress user community, several WordPress forums and tutorials to help us find answers to our questions.

Let us now move ahead and see how WordPress is installed.

1.3 Installing WordPress

For the purpose of blogging, we can install WordPress either on a local web server or on commercial web host. However, there is one more way that relieves us from downloading or installing any software and does everything automatically, that is, by using the free hosted version of WordPress available at WordPress.com. So, in all, there are three possible ways of creating a blog in WordPress:

- Local installation
- Using free hosted version at WordPress.com
- Installing on commercial web hosts

1.3.1 Local installation

WordPress requires a web server with PHP support, a URL rewriting module and an instance of MySQL. The URL rewriting module that understands .htaccess directives is required for the purpose of getting search engine friendly URLs. WordPress generates search engine friendly URLs also called permalinks through URL rewriting modules. Hence, the servers such as Apache or IIS7 providing URL rewriting are popularly used for installing WordPress.

The installation process is quite simple. We need a server software (MAMP, XAMP or WAMP) and a WordPress package (download it from wordpress.org) and follow the below given steps:

Note: WordPress is licensed under the GNU Public License (GPL) version 2.

1. Install a local server (Mac: MAMP, PC:XAMPP or WAMP). Figure 1.1 displays XAMPP control panel that automatically appears on successful installation of XAMPP. We can see that Apache and MySQL both are in running mode.

   Note: Mac OS X comes with an Apache web server (with PHP and URL rewriting).

Figure 1.1 XAMPP Control Panel

2. Next, we have to create a new database. Select the *Admin* button besides *MySQL* from XAMPP control panel to open *phpMyAdmin*. In the *Create new database* textbox, enter the name of the new database as *wordpress_local* (any) followed by selecting the *Create* button as shown in Figure 1.2. After creating the database, the next thing we have to do is to set the password of the *root*. We will be using the user, *root* (that has all the privileges by default) to access the newly created database. By default, when we install XAMPP, there is no password set for the *root*. To set the password of the *root*, select *Privileges* link from the top (Figure 1.2). We get a *User overview* page displaying

the list of default users. Select the *Edit privileges* icon for the *root* on *localhost*. We get a box to specify password for the root. Lets enter the password for the root as *mce* (any text)

Note: The *phpMyAdmin* is a free software tool written in PHP that manages the administration of MySQL over the World Wide Web. It helps us perform variety of database manipulation tasks quite easily.

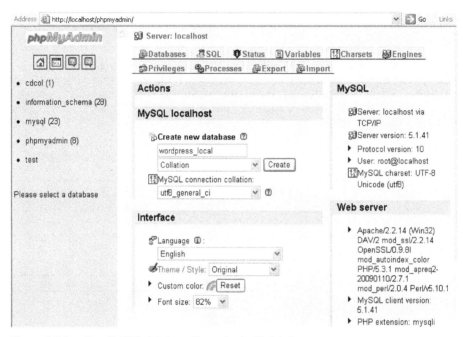

Figure 1.2 Creating MySQL database through phpMyAdmin

3. Extract the downloaded WordPress package in a folder say *blog* (or any other name). Copy the *blog* folder containing the WordPress files into the root directory of our server, i.e., in its *htdocs* folder.

4. In the *blog* folder, we will see that besides other files, WordPress package provides a template configuration file also. The configuration file is named *wp-config-sample.php*. First, we have to rename the *wp-config-sample.php* file to *wp-config.php* and then update it to specify the information (db_name, user, password, host) of the newly created database, *wordpress_local* in it. Hence, open the *wp-config.php* file and search for the following three lines:

```
define('DB_NAME', 'database_name_here');

define('DB_USER', 'username_here');

define('DB_PASSWORD', 'password_here');
```

and modify them to appear as shown below:

```
define('DB_NAME', 'wordpress_local');

define('DB_USER', 'root');

define('DB_PASSWORD', 'mce');
```

where *wordpress_local* is the database we just created through phpMyAdmin, *root* is the default user with all privileges and *mce* is the password that we have set for the root through phpMyAdmin. Save the *wp-config.php* file after making these changes.

5. Open the browser and point it at the URL, http://localhost/blog/wp-admin/install.php to begin the WordPress installation process. The word, *blog* appears in the URL because we have renamed the WordPress package directory to *blog* before copying it on our web server's root directory. On doing this, we get a Welcome page asking information for the blog that we want to create. The page represents the beginning of the WordPress's *five minute installation* process. We enter the title of the blog, name, password and email address of the administrator in the respective textboxes as shown in Figure 1.3. Also, select the checkbox, *Allow my site to appear in search engines like Google and Technorati* if we are making a blog that is open for public and finally select the *Install WordPress* button.

Figure 1.3 Page showing WordPress's five minute installation process

We get a *Success* message (Figure 1.4) declaring that WordPress is successfully installed on our local server. If we enter administrator's name and password and select the *Log In* button, the Dashboard of our blog opens up to administer our blog. Later in this chapter, we will understand Dashboard and its role in administering a blog.

Figure 1.4 Page confirming successful installation of WordPress

To visit our newly created blog, open the browser and point it at the address, http://localhost/blog/. Our blog is displayed with a default post, *Hello world!* provided by WordPress as shown in Figure 1.5.

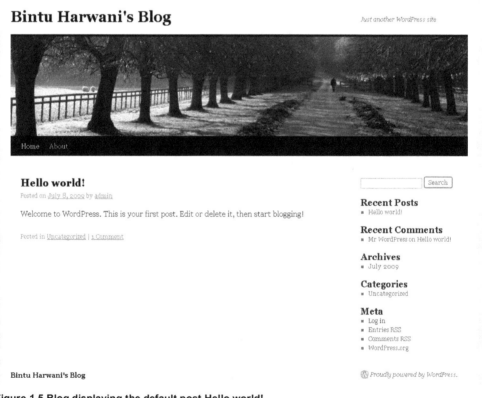

Figure 1.5 Blog displaying the default post Hello world!

In order to open the login page again, point the browser to the following address, `http://localhost/blog/wp-login.php`

1.3.2 Using Free Hosted version at WordPress.com

If you are not interested in purchasing a domain name and hosting your site, `WordPress.com` provides an alternative, that is, `WordPress.com` provides us a free hosting service. That is, we do not have to download any software or install anything; instead everything is done automatically. However, to use the free hosting service, we need to create a `WordPress.com` account.

Let us see how to create a WordPress.com account.

To create your `WordPress.com` user account, follow these steps:

1. Go to the URL `http://wordpress.com`

2. Select the *Sign Up Now!* button. On doing this, you will be asked to fill up a Sign Up form (Figure 1.6).

3. Specify the *Username* and *password*. In the *Username* textbox, enter the name that you will be using for logging into the blog to administer it. In the *Email Address* box, enter the email address; this email address is used by `WordPress.com` for informing us when some action takes place like a post is commented, a post or page is linked, visitor registers to our blog etc. Select the check box in the *Legal Flotsam* section to make the `WordPress.com` folks know that we have read its terms of service. Select either *Gimme a Blog!* option or *Just a Username, Please*. The *Gimme a Blog!* option signs up with a `WordPress.com` account and also sets up a new `WordPress.com` blog. The option, *Just a Username, Please* just signs up with a new WordPress.com account, without the blog setup. Since, we are interested in setting up a new `WordPress.com` blog, we will select the option, *Gimme a Blog!* followed by selecting the *Next* button.

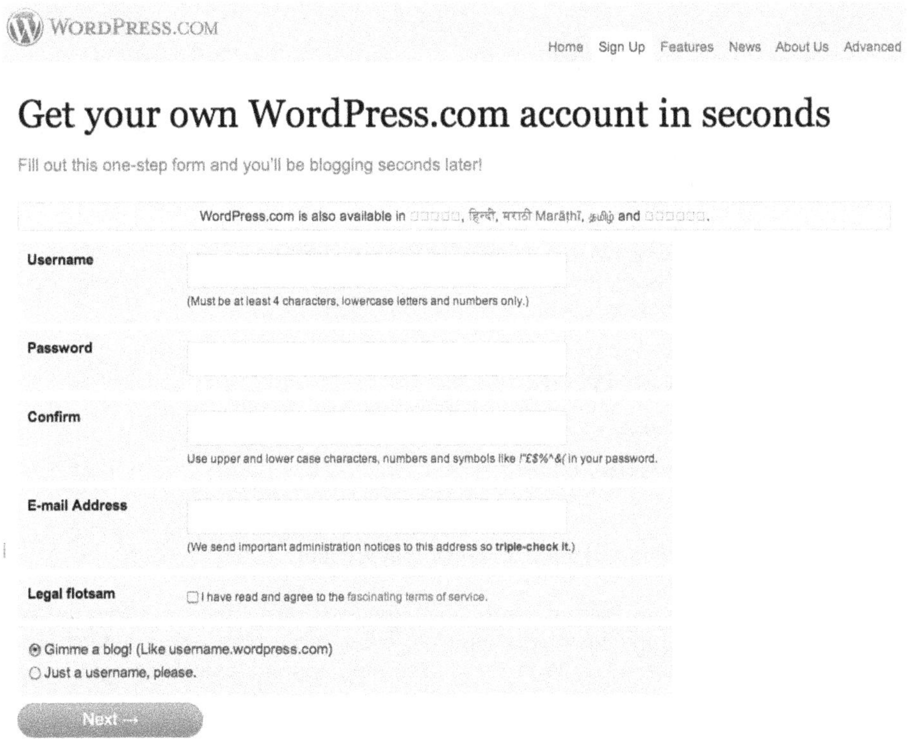

Figure 1.6 Sign Up form to create WordPress.com account

4. We now get a page (Figure 1.7) asking information about the new blog that we want to create. In the *Blog Domain* text box, enter the blog domain name. Whatever we enter here becomes the URL address of our blog. For example, if I enter *bintuharwani* in the *Blog Domain* box, then the URL of my blog will be http://bintuharwani.wordpress.com. The domain name of our blog does not have to be the same as the username. It is better to use a domain name that relates to our site's content. In the *Blog Title* textbox, enter the name for our blog. Select the language that we will be using for blogging from the *Language* drop-down menu. Select the *Public* radio button if we want our blog to be public. Select the *Private* radio button if we want our blog to be private. Select the *Signup* button, and your blog is created.

Figure 1.7 Page asking for information about the newly created blog

5. A new page titled, *Check Your E-mail to Complete Registration* appears on the screen displaying a message that WordPress.com has sent us an e-mail containing a link to activate our account. A form is also displayed below the message allowing us to update our profile. We can use the form to enter first name, last name and some information about ourselves followed by the *Save Profile* button.

6. In the e-mail sent by WordPress.com, we find a link to activate our new WordPress.com blog. The email also contains our username, password and some links that are helpful in blogging. On selecting the link, we get a page saying that our blog is now active as shown in Figure 1.8.

Figure 1.8 Message confirming activation of our Wordpress.com account

The *Login* link visible in the figure, allows us to enter the username and password to login and administer our blog. On selecting the *View your site* link, we see our blog with a default post, *Hello world!* which is automatically published by WordPress. The blog appears exactly as we saw in Figure 1.5.

Note: To log into the blog for administering it, visit the URL, http://wordpress.com and fill in the username and password in the top-left corner of the WordPress.com website.

We will find some limitations while using the free hosted version of WordPress.com. For example, we cannot install plugins, custom themes, customize base code files, access the underlying MySQL databases, etc. Even with these limitations, using the free hosted version is a popular choice among beginners.

1.3.3 Installing WordPress on commercial web hosts

Most of the hosting service providers make the WordPress installation procedure quite simple by providing *Fantastico* application installer in their control panel. On selecting the *Fantastico* icon in our host's control panel, we get a list of applications that *Fantastico* can install for us. On selecting *WordPress* from the list of applications, we get a screen displaying information of package being installed as shown in Figure 1.9. This page displays a small description of WordPress, its version, the amount of disk space required and a link for support forum.

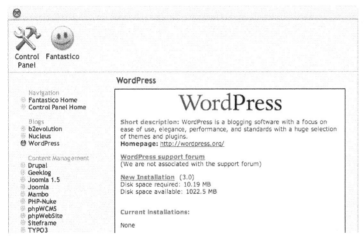

Figure 1.9 Using Fantastico tool for installing WordPress

On selecting the *New Installation* link, we are asked to specify the following:

- the domain where we want to install WordPress,
- the directory where we want to install WordPress,
- administrator's username, password, nickname and email address, and
- the website's name and its description.

Let us enter the asked information as shown in Figure 1.10.

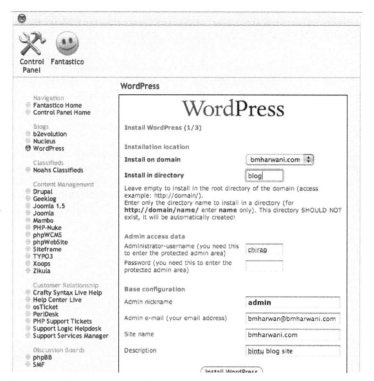

Figure 1.10 Page to enter information related to WordPress installation

Assuming we want to install WordPress on the domain, bmharwani.com, let us select, bmharwani.com from the *Install on domain* drop down menu. To install WordPress in a separate directory say *blog* (and not in the root directory), we enter *blog* in the *Install in directory* text box. If the main directory provided by our web host is *public_html*, then the WordPress is installed in a directory *blog* inside the main directory *public_html*. It also means that our blog is accessible through the address http://bmharwani.com/blog

Note: If we want our blog's URL to be bmharwani.com instead of bmharwani.com/blog, we will leave the *Install in directory* (refer to Figure 1.10) textbox empty thus installing WordPress in the main directory.

After entering the desired information, we initiate WordPress installation by selecting the *Install WordPress* button. On doing this, WordPress is installed and MySQL database and user is created automatically. We are now asked to complete the installation process by selecting the *Finish* installation button as shown in Figure 1.11.

Figure 1.11 Page to finish the WordPress installation on a commercial web host

Note: Fantastico will automatically create MySQL database and a MySQL user that is used in the WordPress installation.

Let us see if our blog is created. Open the browser and point it at the address, http://bmharwani.com/blog. Our blog appears with a default post *Hello world!* provided by WordPress as shown in Figure 1.12.

bmharwani.com

bintu blog site

Home   About

Search

Hello world!

Posted on September 12, 2010 by chintu

Welcome to WordPress. This is your first post. Edit or delete it, then start blogging!

This entry was posted in Uncategorized. Bookmark the permalink.

Recent Posts
- Hello world!

Recent Comments
- Mr WordPress on Hello world!

Archives
- September 2010

Categories
- Uncategorized

Meta
- Log in
- Entries RSS
- Comments RSS
- WordPress.org

Figure 1.12 Front page of the blog displaying the default post, Hello world!

Note: By Default, WordPress creates a Post and a Page for us. The Post is titled Hello world! and the Page is titled About.

We can see in Figure 1.12 that at the top of the page, above the image, is the title of the website that we had defined while installation. The black area just under the image is the navigation menu. At the moment, the navigation menu displays two links, *Home* and *About*. We can add more custom menus to our blog. Below the header and the menu, there are two columns: the *content area* and the *sidebar*. The *content area* shows the most recent blog posts. This site's sidebar displays six widgets by default: *Search, Recent Posts, Recent Comments, Archives, Categories* and *Meta*. These six widgets are displayed with default themes. Additional widgets may appear in different themes as few themes and plugins result in displaying more widgets.

To administer our blog, we need to log in. The login page appears as shown in Figure 1.13. on pointing the browser at the following address: `http://bmharwani.com/blog/wp-login.php`.

Figure 1.13 WordPress login page

Logging in to the blog takes us to the *Dashboard* page—a steering page of our blog. On the left-hand side of the Dashboard page is the main navigation menu. Before we discuss about the kind of information displayed via Dashboard page, let us first have an idea of the main navigation menu.

1.4 Main Navigation Menu

Main navigation menu is a collection of ten different menus (refer to Figure 1.14(a)) and appears on all the pages along the left-hand side of the browser window. Each menu in the main navigation menu displays an icon and text and has an arrow to the right of it. On clicking the arrow, the menu expands to show its options, i.e., submenu. Clicking the arrow again collapses the submenu. On selecting the small arrow dividers between sections, the main navigation menu switches to the icons only, hover-style menu as shown in Figure 1.14(b).

| (a) | (b) |

Figure 1.14 (a) Icons and texts of menus in Main Navigation Menu (b) Icons of menus in Main Navigation Menu

We get back the menu text on selecting the arrow dividers again. The brief description of the usage of different menus displayed in the main navigation menu is given in Table 1.1.

Table 1.1 Brief description of different menus of the Main navigation menu

Menu	Used To
Posts	Manage posts of our website. To update our visitors, to inform about the new event or launch of the new product, etc. is done by publishing posts on our site.
Media	Manage the media of our website such as images, video, audio recordings and files that are uploaded on the site.
Links	Manage links and links categories (blogroll) of the website.
Pages	Display static content on our website.
Comments	Manage comments. We can easily approve, reply, edit and delete comments.
Plugins	Manage plugins. In order to extend functionality of our website, we install plugins to our site which are in the form of codes that interact with the WordPress API.
Users	Manage user accounts, which includes, creating user accounts, assigning roles and defining profiles. Roles are the easiest way of controlling access to our website.
Tools	Manage content of our website, i.e., allowing us to import and export contents of our website.
Settings	Configure various features and functionality on our website.

Lets now have a look at the type of information displayed by Dashboard.

1.5 Dashboard

The Dashboard is the first thing that we come across when we log into our blog. It displays an overview of statistical information about the site and some updates about WordPress development and plugins. We get several boxes known as *Widgets* on the Dashboard such as *Right Now, Recent Comments, Incoming Links, QuickPress, Recent Drafts*, etc. that are used to configure our blog. By default, the widgets are displayed in two columns as shown in Figure 1.15.

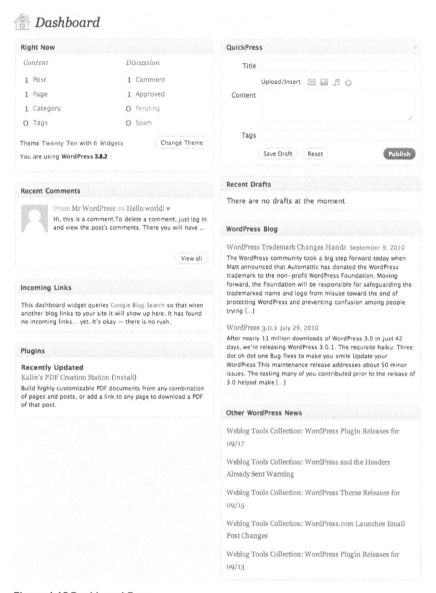

Figure 1.15 Dashboard Page

The widgets displayed on the Dashboard provide various information and functionality for administering our blog. The list of widgets that are displayed in Dashboard by default is as under:

- **Right Now Widget**—It shows top-level statistics regarding the blog's content. It shows the number of posts, pages, category, tags, comments and even spam that are present in our website. Clicking on any statistic navigates us to the page for managing that content. Below the blog's statistics, the Right Now widget displays the theme that is currently active in our blog with the total number of widgets. The current WordPress version is also displayed and in case a new version of WordPress is available, a button appears allowing us to update the version.

- **Recent Comments Widget**—It displays most recent comments published on our blog. WordPress displays a maximum of five comments in this box. The name of the commenter also appears along with her picture or avatar, if any.

- **Incoming Links Widget**—This Widget displays the list of sites that are linked to our blog. This widget uses Google Blog Search (http://blogsearch.google.com/) to find incoming links to our blog. If any incoming links exist, they are displayed here in the reverse chronological order, showing the most recent one at the top.

- **Plugins Widget**—It is an RSS widget that displays the news of the plugins. For example, it displays the current most popular plugin, the newest plugin or the recently updated plugins, and so on.

- **QuickPress Widget**—It is used to create a new blog post quickly right from the Dashboard. We can fill in the title and content of the post, upload and insert image(s), or other media and finally, either save the post as a draft or publish it on our blog. There are certain limitations in creating a post from this widget, for example, we can use tags but not categories, cannot change the post's publication date or status, etc.

- **Recent Drafts Widget**—It shows the posts that are not ready to publish and are in draft mode, i.e., some work is still pending on them.

- **WordPress Blog Widget**—It is an RSS widget that contains news and information regarding the development of WordPress, new versions of WordPress, etc.

- **Other WordPress News Widget**—It is also an RSS widget that displays a collection of WordPress related blogs featuring news and information regarding all its aspects.

The three RSS widgets (Plugins, WordPress Blog and Other WordPress News) can be changed to display any RSS feed. Just hover over the title and click on the Edit link that appears and change the feed to any RSS feed we like and Save. This helps us display any RSS feed content directly on our WordPress Dashboard.

1.6 Summary

In this chapter, we got an overview of different blogging platforms along with an introduction to WordPress and its features. We also saw different installation methods of WordPress. Finally, we got an idea of different menus in the man navigation menu and different types of information displayed by Dashboard.

The next chapter is focused on creating and managing our blog contents, that is, creating Posts and Pages for our blog.

2

Posts and Pages

In this chapter, we will learn to create and manage the contents of our website. Posts and pages are the two important ways to create content for our visitors. So we need to explain the difference between the two.

Posts are the dynamic contents that we publish to update the visitors of our website. For example, information about a new event or launch of a new product would be delivered through posts. Posts are always associated with a date. Pages, on the other hand, refer to static contents of our website that are not frequently updated. For example, the information in About Us and Contact Us are delivered in the form of Pages.

Let's begin with Post creation.

2.1 Posts

Posts menu is meant for managing the contents of our blog. It provides options for adding new posts to our blog, edit contents of the posts and even delete posts. It also helps manage the categories to which these posts are assigned. Apart from this, the post menu also helps us in maintaining tags (also known as keywords) that describe our posts and also helps the reader in locating the posts which have specific content. On selecting Posts menu from the main navigation menu, we get a submenu that shows all the options of the Posts menu as shown in Figure 2.1.

Figure 2.1. Posts menu options

Table 2.1 describes these options.

Table 2.1. Post Menu Options

Option	Usage
Posts	Used for editing, deleting, viewing, and searching posts
Add New	Used for adding news posts to our website
Categories	Used for managing post categories. All the posts on our site must be assigned to a category. Categorizing posts among different categories or subjects provides all related information in one place so visitors of our website don't have to do a lot of searching. Visitors can just click specific categories to see all related posts.
Post Tags	Used for creating, editing, deleting, and searching tags. Tags are used to describe our post and help the search engines to locate our posts.

Before we begin creating contents for our website, we should take some time and decide what categories we are going to publish. If I want to deliver information on different platforms to my visitors by posting few articles, it is better to categorize the articles on the basis of their subjects, for example, Smartphone, PHP, or .NET articles.

So, before creating any post, we'll first create categories for the contents we are going to publish.

2.2 Creating New Categories

To add new categories, open the *Posts* menu and select the *Categories* link. The *Categories* page opens, as shown in Figure 2.2. The left side of the Categories page is the area for adding new category and the right side of the figure is known as *category management area* where we can edit and delete all post categories of our blog. We can also search desired categories (in case the list is long) using the *Search* box at the top right. Upon installation, WordPress provides us with one default category called *Uncategorized*. We can change the name of this default category, if desired. If any post is not assigned to a category, it will be automatically assigned to the default category.

Figure 2.2. Add New Category page

Type the name of the new category in the *Name* text box and type a name in the *Slug* text box. The slug creates the link to the category page that lists all the posts submitted in this category. If we leave this field blank, WordPress will automatically create a slug based on the category name. The slug is created by converting the category name into lower case and replacing spaces by hyphens. For example, if the category is Smartphone Articles, WordPress will create the slug as
http://example.com/category/smartphone-articles.

We can also refine our category with subcategories. Subcategories lists specific topics related to the main category. The subcategories are listed directly below the main category. To create a subcategory, we need to select the main category from the *Parent* drop-down menu. Assuming a category called *Gadgets* is already created, we can make the category *Smartphone Articles* a subcategory of *Gadgets* by selecting *Gadgets* from the *Parent* drop-down. Because we want the category *Smartphone Article* to be a top level category and not a subcategory of some other category, we choose *None* from the *Parent* drop-down menu.

In the *Description* text box, type a small description of the category to remind us what the category is all about. Finally, select the *Add New Category* button to create a new category. Categories can be sorted by WordPress in two ways: by name (alphabetically), or by ID number. As we add new categories, each is automatically assigned an ID number by WordPress that is difficult to change. So it's better to create categories in the order we want to see them appear on our website.

Note: We can add an unlimited number of categories to our website.

Let's say that we we'll be writing about Smartphones on our blog and want to create an independent category called *Smartphone Articles*. To create a category, we enter information in following respective fields, which were shown in Figure 2.2:

- **Name**—Smartphone Articles
- **Slug**—smartphone-articles
- **Parent**—None
- **Description**—Article related to iPhone, Android, Blackberry, iPad, and so on.

After entering the information above, we select *Add New Category* button and find the newly added category, *Smartphone Articles,* in the category management area on the right side of the page, as shown in Figure 2.3.

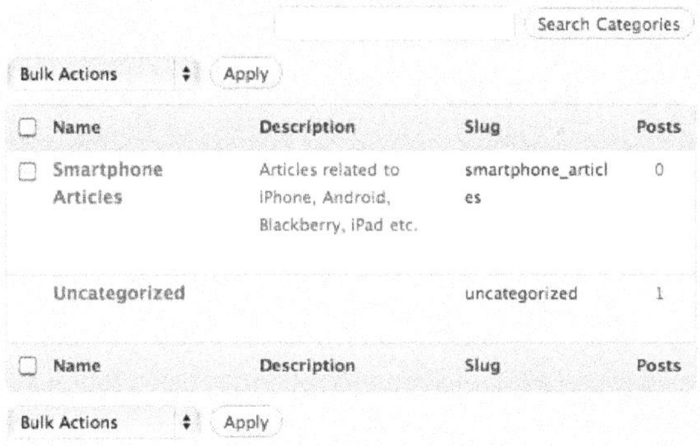

				Search Categories

Bulk Actions	⬍	Apply		
☐ Name		Description	Slug	Posts
☐ Smartphone Articles		Articles related to iPhone, Android, Blackberry, iPad etc.	smartphone_articl es	0
Uncategorized			uncategorized	1
☐ Name		Description	Slug	Posts

Bulk Actions ⬍ Apply

Figure 2.3. The newly added category, Smartphone Articles, appears in the category management area

The number *0* and *1* in the Smartphone Articles *Posts* column says that currently, there is no post in *Smartphone Articles* category and one post in the *Uncategorized* category. Remember that WordPress creates a default post titled *Hello world!* on installation and assigns it to the *Uncategorized* category .

Note: We may not see our newly added category on our blog sidebars, because WordPress doesn't displays a category until a single post has been assigned to it. So, when we add a post to the newly created category, it will appear on our blog

---

To delete or edit a category, hover over the category title and several links will appear below the category title: *Edit, Quick Edit*, and *Delete*. Clicking the *Delete* link will delete that category from WordPress. Deleting a category doesn't delete the posts and links in that category. Instead, posts in the deleted category are assigned to the *Uncategorized* default . The *Quick Edit* link allows us to edit the category name and slug, but not the parent and description of the category. The *Edit* link allows us to modify all the four fields.

If we select the *Quick Edit* link of our newly added *Smartphone Articles* category, we'll see the screen to edit the category's name and slug, as shown in Figure 2.4.

Figure 2.4. Quick Edit box for categories

After changing the category name, we can save the changes by selecting the *Update Category* button. We don't want to make any changes, so let's select *Cancel* button instead.

We can also convert some or all of the categories of our blog to tags by selecting the *Category to Tag Converter* link in the *category management area* (see Figure 2.2). The difference between categories and tags is that the categories are used for organizing the posts, whereas tags are used for describing the posts. The categories can be hierarchical, that is, categories can have sub-categories, and sub-sub categories, but tags cannot. Converting categories to tags and vice versa is explained in the next chapter. We will learn about tags in detail in the *Post Tags* section later on in the chapter.

Note: Tags are the comma-separated keywords that describe our posts. They define the topics inside our posts and help search engines locate our posts, because Search-engine spiders harvest tags when they crawl around the Web.

2.3 Editing Categories

To edit a category, we either click the category title in the *category management area* (see Figure 2.3) or select the *Edit* link that appears when the mouse hovers over the category title. For example, let's select the *Uncategorized* category and see that the *Edit Category* page will open. Let's modify the name of the Uncategorized category to *General*, as shown in Figure 2.5.

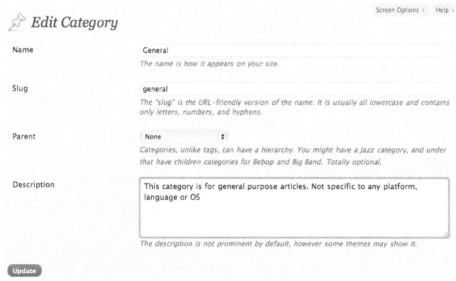

Figure 2.5. Modifying the default category

While editing a category, we can type a new name for the category in the *Name* text box and enter a new slug in the *Slug* text box. In the *Description* text box, we can type a summary of the category. To apply and save the changes made, we need to select *Update* button.

To change Uncategorized to General, make the following changes:

- In the *Name* text box, enter the name of the category as General.
- Enter the slug as general in *Slug* text box.
- Choose the *None* option from the *Parent* drop-down menu, because we want *General* to be an independent category and not a subcategory.
- In the *Description* box, enter a brief description of the category.
- Select *Update* button to save the changes.

After selecting the *Update* button, the *Categories* page will reload, showing the new category name on the right side of the page in the category management area.

Note: Regardless of the name assigned to the Uncategorized category, it will still be considered as the default, and all unassigned posts will be assigned to this default category.

Since, we have enough knowledge of categories, we can go ahead and write and submit posts for our blog

2.4 Managing Posts

When the *Posts* option is selected from the *Posts* menu, we see a *post management* screen, as shown in Figure 2.6. The *post management* screen displays all the posts of our website in tabular format. At the moment, we find a *Hello world!* post, which was published for us by WordPress. The *Hello world!* post is assigned to *Uncategorized* category by default. In the last section, we modified the *Uncategorized* category to *General*, hence Figure 2.6 shows the *Hello world!* post assigned to the General category.

In the *post management* screen, we find several links across the top that can filter our posts on the basis of their status. To view all posts in *Draft* status, just click the *Draft* link at the top. Similarly, to see all published posts, select the *Published* link at the top. To view all the posts, select the *All* link. At the moment, we see only two filter links, All and Published, but two more links, *Draft* and *Trash,* will be added to the filter links when a post is deleted or saved as a draft.

We can also search all posts for specific keywords using the *Search box* at the top-right. The *Show all dates* drop-down is used to list posts that were published on the specified date. Similarly, the *View all categories* drop-down is used to list all the posts of the specified category. To edit or delete several posts simultaneously, you can use of *Bulk Actions* drop-down menu.

Bulk Actions—The Bulk Actions drop-down is used to edit or delete multiple posts simultaneously. All, we need to do is select the checkboxes of the post(s) to which we want to apply a bulk action and select the desired action from the *Bulk Actions* drop-down menu. After selecting an action, click the *Apply* button to execute the action.

Posts are displayed in a *List* view by default, but we can also display them in an *Excerpt* view by selecting either the *List* or *Excerpt* view icon located below the search box. The *Excerpt* view shows all the posts along with an excerpt of the post.

Figure 2.6. Posts Management screen

When the mouse is hovered over a post, four links appear below the post title, Edit, Quick Edit, Trash and View. These links are explained here:

- **Edit**—Opens the Edit Post page to apply modifications to the post

- **Quick Edit**—Allows you quick access to post information. The post information is loaded through AJAX, and hence there is no need of page refresh to see the changes applied. We can edit everything from this link except the contents of the post.

- **Trash**—Deletes the post from our website. Before deleting the post, WordPress asks for confirmation.

- **View**—Displays the post as it will appear to the visitor.

To add a new Post, select the *Add New* button. We'll see a page to add new post to our website.

2.5 Add New Post

The *Add New Post* page opens either when the *Add New* button is clicked in the post management screen or by selecting *Posts->Add New* option from the main navigation menu. The page appears as shown in Figure 2.7 .

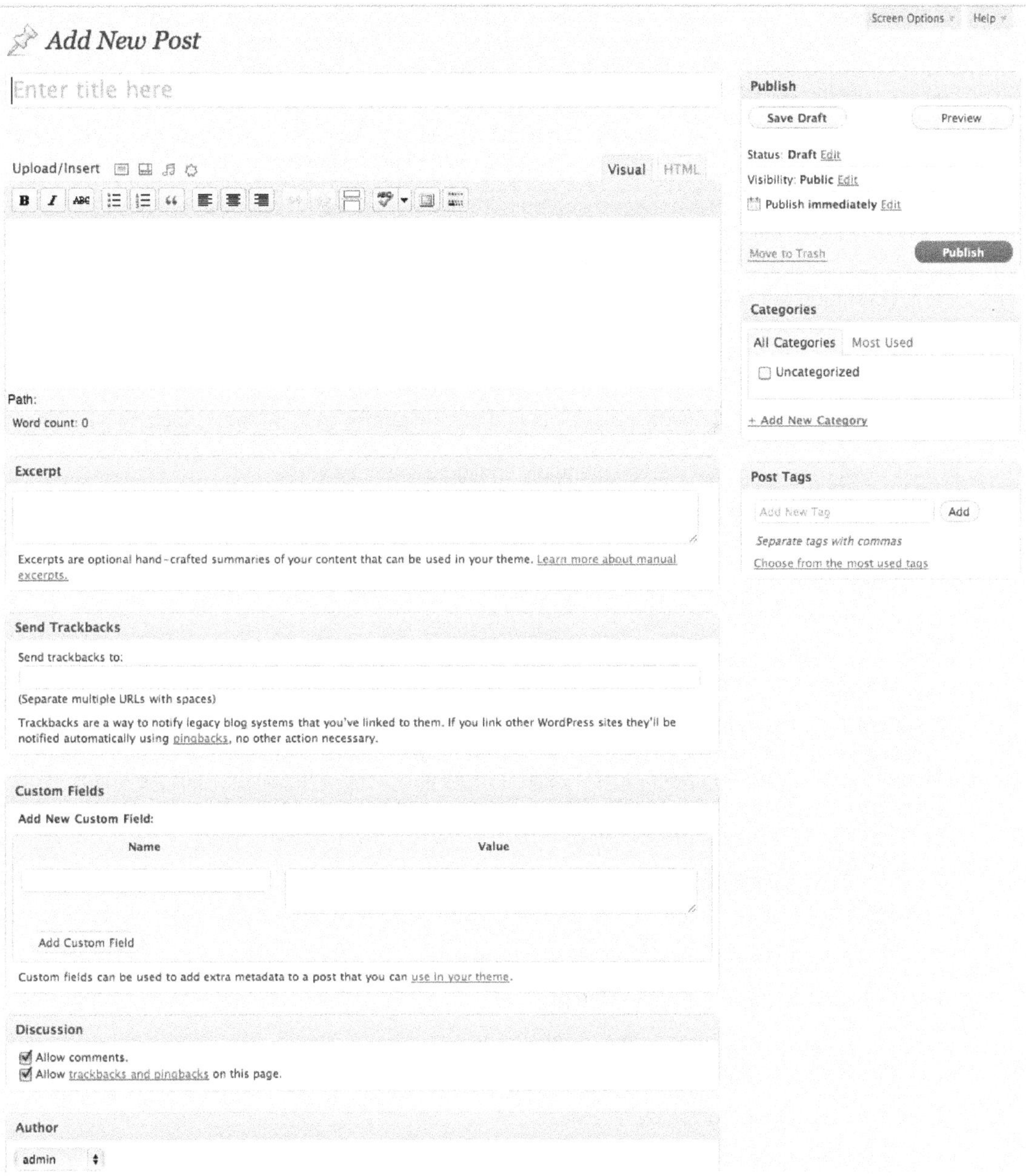

Add New Post

Screen Options ▾   Help ▾

Enter title here

Publish

Save Draft   Preview

Status: **Draft** Edit
Visibility: **Public** Edit
Publish immediately Edit

Move to Trash   **Publish**

Upload/Insert   Visual   HTML

B *I* ABC ≔ ≔ ❝ ▤ ▤ ▤   ▤ ▼ ▤ ▤

Categories

All Categories   Most Used

☐ Uncategorized

+ Add New Category

Path:
Word count: 0

Post Tags

Add New Tag   Add

Separate tags with commas
Choose from the most used tags

Excerpt

Excerpts are optional hand-crafted summaries of your content that can be used in your theme. Learn more about manual excerpts.

Send Trackbacks

Send trackbacks to:

(Separate multiple URLs with spaces)

Trackbacks are a way to notify legacy blog systems that you've linked to them. If you link other WordPress sites they'll be notified automatically using pingbacks, no other action necessary.

Custom Fields

Add New Custom Field:

Name	Value

Add Custom Field

Custom fields can be used to add extra metadata to a post that you can use in your theme.

Discussion

☑ Allow comments.
☑ Allow trackbacks and pingbacks on this page.

Author

admin   ▼

Figure 2.7. Add New Post screen

The usage of the textboxes and tabs found in Figure 2.7 is as follows:

- **Post title box**—Enter the title of the new post in the Post title box. Commas, apostrophes, quotes, hyphens, dashes, and other punctuation are allowed. To make the title search-engine friendly, WordPress will clean special symbols from the post link, if necessary.

- **Post content box**—Write the content of the post in the Post content box. The contents may include text and links. We can use either the Visual or HTML mode to compose the post and insert media, such as images, videos, and PDFs, via the four icons located next to *Upload/Insert* icon located below the Title text box. The icons represent image, video, sound, and media respectively. Inserted images appear in the post only in Visual view. We can select the image, adjust its alignment, apply image settings, and delete the image from the post, if necessary. In HTML view, you'll only see HTML IMG tags,

- **Excerpt box**—Write a short summary of the post in this box. This text is optional, but useful, as it appears on the front page of our site and let's the visitor know what the post is about.

  Note: The Excerpt does not appear by default. To make it appear in our post, we have to change the index.php template file to display the Excerpt instead of the full Content of a post. WordPress will automatically use the first 55 words of our post as the Excerpt.

- **Send Trackbacks**—This setting is used to notify legacy blog systems that we have linked to them. When we link other WordPress blogs, they are automatically notified via pingbacks. For the blogs that don't recognize pingbacks, we can send a trackback to the blog by entering the website address in this box. If there is more than one website, the addresses are separated by a space.

- **Custom Fields**—Custom Fields are used to add extra information to our post, such as providing custom CSS for the post, expiry date of the post, and an image of the post. The custom fields are usually used by plugins, but we can manually configure them, as well.

- **Discussion**—Discussion is used to enable interactivity and notification of our posts. It contains two checkboxes: *Allow Comments* and *Allow trackbacks and pingbacks on this page*. If the *Allow Comments* checkbox is unchecked, no one can post comments to this particular post. *If Allow trackbacks and pingbacks on this page* checkbox is unchecked, no one can post pingbacks or trackbacks to this particular post.

- **Author**—The drop-down list displays a list of blog authors. Here, we can select a name to use as the post author. .

- **Publish tab**—In the Publish tab, we can select the *Save Draft* button to temporarily save the post so we can work on it later. Drafts are not published on the website. The *Preview* button is used to see how the new post will appear to the visitors when published. We can also set the status of our Post by selecting the *Edit* link next to *Status*. The post can have any of the following states: *Published, Pending Review*, and *Draft*.

  - The *Published* status means the post is published on the website for the visitors to see.

  - The *Pending Review* status means the draft has to be viewed by an editor before it is published.

  - Draft status means the post is not yet complete.

  To apply a specific publish status to the post, select the desired publish status and click the *Update* button.
  The visibility of the Post can be set by selecting *Edit* link next to *Visibility*. We can make the post appear as *Public, Password protected* and *Private :*

  - *Public* posts can be viewed by all visitors.

  - *Password Protected* posts will be visible to the visitors who know the password.

  - *Private* posts are visible to the admin and editor of the blog.

  Finally, we can publish to the Post by selecting *Publish* button or delete it completely by selecting *Move to Trash* link. When we select *Publish* button, the post becomes visible to visitors of our website and its publication date is set to the current date and time. To change the date, select the *Edit* link next to *Publish immediately*. Some form fields will appear that we can use to set the desired publication date of the post. If we enter some future date, the post will be scheduled to publish on that date.

- **Categories**—The posts should be categorized into different subjects for the convenience of visitors. Unassigned posts are automatically assigned to the *Uncategorized* category—the default category provided by WordPress. In this area, we can select the checkbox of the category to which we want to assign the new post. We can also select the *Add New Category* link below the *Categories* tab to create a new category. The *Most Used* link displays the categories that are frequently used.

Note: A post can be assigned to multiple categories.

- **Post Tags**—We type tags for the post in this box. The tags are the keywords that describe our post and help the Search Engines in finding the Post. After writing the tags, separated by commas, click *Add* button. When we type in a tag, WordPress automatically suggests tags based on the existing tags. We can also view the most used tags by selecting the *Choose from the most used tags* link.

Note: Posts are displayed in reverse chronological order (latest post at the top) and tags and categories can be assigned to them for search engines.

Let's add a new post to our blog titled *Working with Forms,* and assign it to the category we just created, *Smartphone Articles*. We will select the *Visual* tab before writing the content in the *Post content box*. We can either directly type the contents into the *Post content box* or paste in text from other documents.. In this box, we can also format and align the text, apply bullets, and spell-check by using the icons displayed in the toolbar of *Post content box*.

Assign the post to the *Smartphone Articles* category by selecting its checkbox from the *Categories* tab. We know the tags help search engines in locating our post, so lets add the keywords that describe our new post in the *Post Tags* area. Add tags that relate to the content of our post, for example, *Forms, $_GET, $_POST, $_REQUEST, iPhone web application, web application for Smartphone*. After entering the tags, separated by commas, select the *Add* button to add the tags. The post should look something like that shown in Figure 2.8.

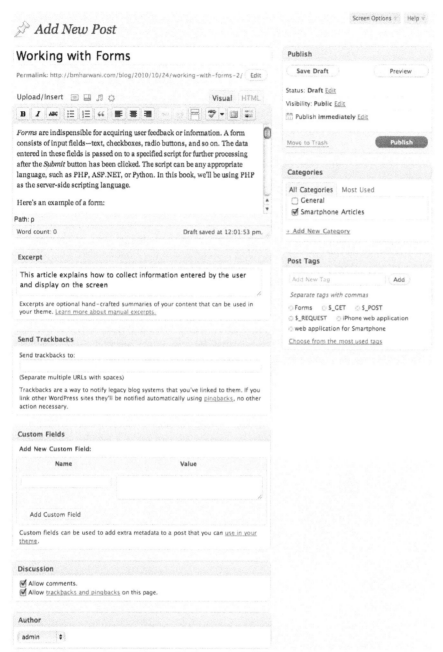

Figure 2.8. Adding the Working with Forms to the blog

We want to add an image to the post. Adding media is explained in detail in later sections, but for now, let's see a quick overview. Place the cursor in the post where we want to insert an image, then select the *Add Image* icon, the first icon above the *Post content box*. We'll see a dialog box to upload an image, as shown in Figure 2.9. The dialog box allows us to upload image(s) from any location, including our local computer, a website or an existing Media Library. The *From Computer* tab is selected by default, allowing us to upload image(s) from our local computer.

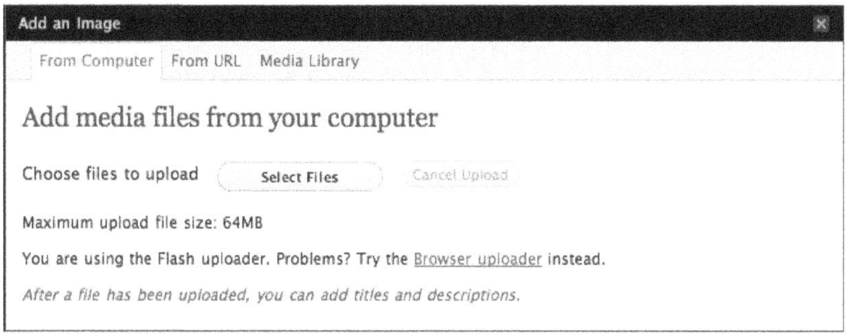

Figure 2.9. Media uploader box

We'll just use the default and click the *Select Files* button to specify the path and name of the image file to be uploaded. After selecting the formfig1.png image, we'll see the screen shown in Figure 2.10.

Figure 2.10. Screen to set properties of the uploaded image

The screen allows us to specify the properties of the selected image, such as *Alternate Text, Caption, Description, Alignment,* and *Size*. For the time being, we will leave all the settings at the default values and select the *Insert into Post* button. The image will be inserted into our post, as shown in Figure 2.11.

Figure 2.11. The Working with Forms post with the inserted image

The final step for publishing the newly added post is to select the *Publish* button. Our post will be published and be visible on our blog, as shown in Figure 2.12.

bmharwani.com   *bintu blog site*

Home   About

(Search)

Working with Forms

Posted on October 24, 2010 by admin

Forms are indispensible for acquiring user feedback or information. A form consists of input fields—text, checkboxes, radio buttons, and so on. The data entered in these fields is passed on to a specified script for further processing after the *Submit* button has been clicked. The script can be any appropriate language, such as PHP, ASP.NET, or Python. In this book, we'll be using PHP as the server-side scripting language.

Here's an example of a form:

```
<form action="createuser.php" method="POST">
```

```
<ul class="rounded">
```

Recent Posts
- Working with Forms
- Hello world!

Recent Comments
- Mr WordPress on Hello world!

Archives
- October 2010
- September 2010

Categories
- General
- Smartphone Articles

Meta
- Log in
- Entries RSS
- Comments RSS
- WordPress.org

Figure 2.12. The newly added post, Working with Forms, appears on the front page of the blog

The latest post appears on the front page by default, so we can see the newly added post, *Working with Forms,* on the front page of the blog. We also see the name of our post under the *Recent Posts* tab. Because the post was added in October, a new link called *October 2010* appears under the *Archives* tab . All posts published in October 2010 will be shown when this link is selected. In the *Categories* tab, we now see two links: *General* and *Smartphone Articles*. The *General* category is the modified name of the default *Uncategorized* category.

Congratulations for successfully publishing a new post to the blog! But the post may need some tweaks, so let's look at the ways we can edit our material.

2.6 Edit Post

Recall that on hovering the mouse over a post in post management screen, four links appear below the post: Title, Edit, Quick Edit, Trash and View. When we select the *Edit* link of a post, it will open in edit mode. Lets open the *Hello world!* post that was provided by WordPress, which should look something like the page shown in Figure 2.13.

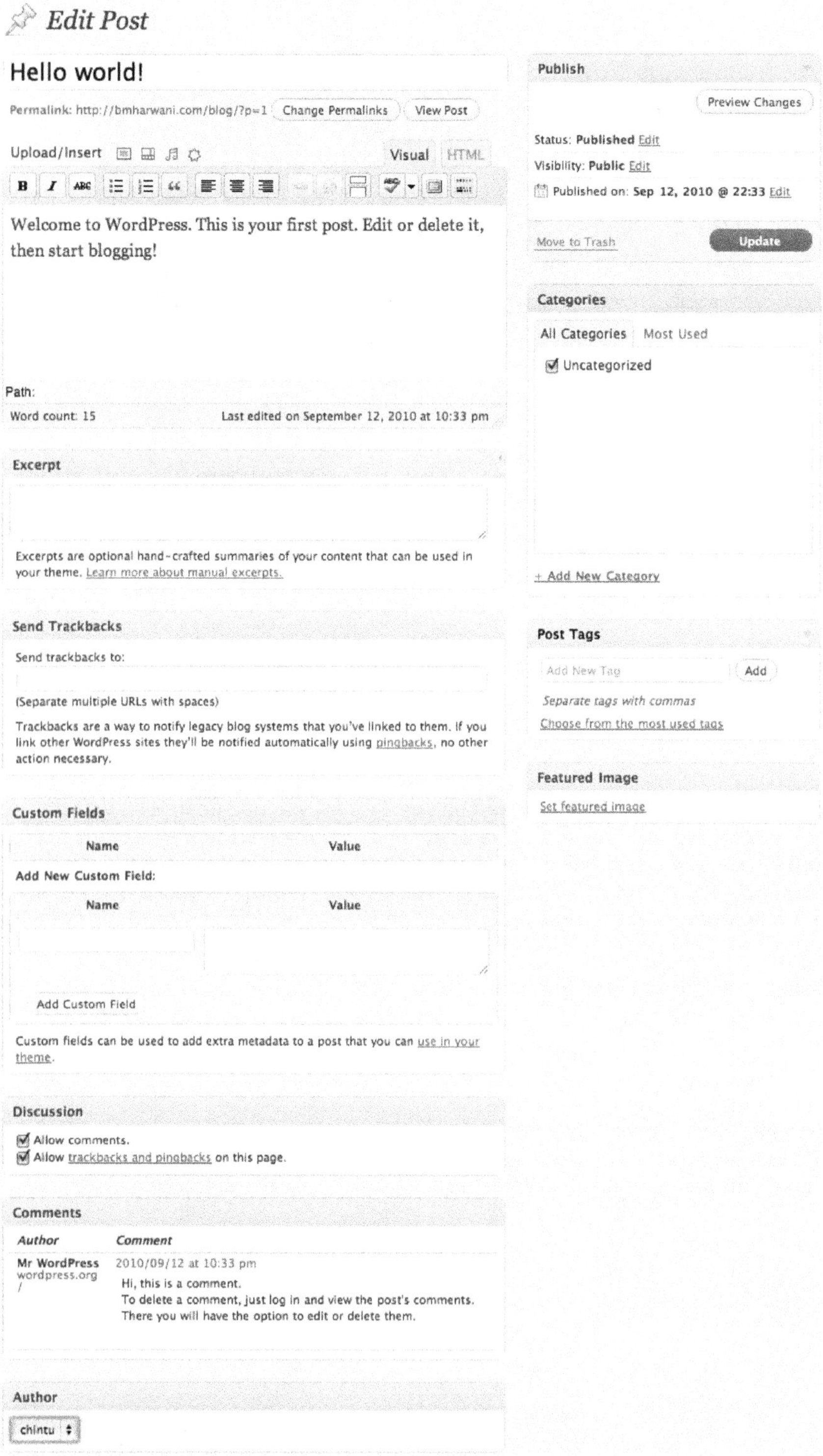

Edit Post

Hello world!

Permalink: http://bmharwani.com/blog/?p=1 (Change Permalinks) (View Post)

Upload/Insert   🖼 🖽 ♫ ○   Visual   HTML

B *I* ABC ≔ ≔ 66 ≡ ≡ ≡   🗏 ✍ ▾ 🖼 ▦

Welcome to WordPress. This is your first post. Edit or delete it, then start blogging!

Path:

Word count: 15   Last edited on September 12, 2010 at 10:33 pm

---

Excerpt

Excerpts are optional hand–crafted summaries of your content that can be used in your theme. Learn more about manual excerpts.

Send Trackbacks

Send trackbacks to:

(Separate multiple URLs with spaces)

Trackbacks are a way to notify legacy blog systems that you've linked to them. If you link other WordPress sites they'll be notified automatically using pingbacks, no other action necessary.

Custom Fields

Name	Value

Add New Custom Field:

Name	Value

    Add Custom Field

Custom fields can be used to add extra metadata to a post that you can use in your theme.

Discussion

☑ Allow comments.
☑ Allow trackbacks and pingbacks on this page.

Comments

Author	Comment
Mr WordPress wordpress.org /	2010/09/12 at 10:33 pm
	Hi, this is a comment.
	To delete a comment, just log in and view the post's comments. There you will have the option to edit or delete them.

Author

[chintu ⬍]

Publish

(Preview Changes)

Status: **Published** Edit

Visibility: **Public** Edit

📅 Published on: **Sep 12, 2010 @ 22:33** Edit

Move to Trash   (**Update**)

Categories

All Categories | Most Used

☑ Uncategorized

+ Add New Category

Post Tags

[Add New Tag] (Add)

Separate tags with commas

Choose from the most used tags

Featured Image

Set featured image

Figure 2.13. The default post, Hello world! in Edit mode

Let's take a look at the different fields in the Edit Post page.

- **Title**—Used to edit title of the post.

- **Change Permalinks**—Used to change the permalinks. To identify the post, WordPress automatically generates permalinks, also known as a *post-slug,* for the post while saving it. By default, the permalinks generated are not search-engine friendly. We will learn about generating search-engine friendly permalinks in Chapter 7.

- **View Post**—Displays the post on the website.

- **Post Editing Area**—Displays the post contents for editing.

- **Excerpt Area**—Used to edit a post excerpt.

- **Send Trackbacks**—Used to edit the URLs of the blog(s) we want to notify that we have linked to them.

- **Custom Fields**—Used to edit the custom fields that we added to provide extra information of the post.

- **Discussion**—Used to either allow or disallow the visitors to write comments on the posts and to send trackbacks and pingbacks about this post.

- **Comments**—Used to edit or delete the post comments.

- **Author**—Used to change the post author.

- **Publish box**—Used to change the status, visibility, and publication date of the post. The post can have any of the following visibility settings: Public, Password Protected, or Private. The *Edit* link next to *Published On* is used to change the publication date of the post.

  - **Preview Changes** —Allows us to view the post before publishing it.

  - **Update**—Used to save and update the post settings.

- **Categories**—Used to change the post category. To add a new category, click the *+Add New Category* link in this section.

- **Post Tags**—Used to edit the post tags. The tags describe the post and also help the search engines in locating our post. We can also add new tags by just typing new tags, separated by commas, into the box and clicking *Add* button.

- **Featured Image**—Some WordPress themes use an image to represent each post. The image will be displayed on the front page and the blog page, and in archives. We can specify a thumbnail image of our post by clicking the *Set Featured Image* link under the *Featured Image* tab. Then we select the uploaded image as the featured image of this post.

2.7 Delete Post

Because we don't want the default *Hello world!* post anymore, there's no point in editing it. Lets see how to delete the post, *Hello world!* from our blog.

We first need to open the post management screen. From the *Edit Post* page, we go back to the post management screen by selecting *Posts->Post* option from main navigation menu. In the post management screen, when we hover the mouse over any post, four links appear below the title of the post, *Edit, Quick Edit, Trash* and *View*. To delete the post, hover the mouse over it and, from the links that appear below the title, select the *Trash* link. The post will immediately disappear from our blog. The *General* category (see Figure 2.12) to which the *Hello world!* post belonged, will also disappear because it is empty.

Note: WordPress displays a category only if at least one post is assigned to it.

When the post is deleted, another filter link, *Trash (1)* appears, as shown in Figure 2.14. The (1) now shows a single post in the trash.

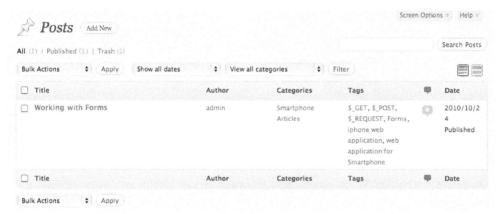

Figure 2.14. The Trash link showing the number of posts sent to Trash

When the *Trash* link is selected, we see a screen showing all the posts that are in trash at the moment, as shown in Figure 2.15. As expected, there is only one post in the trash, *Hello world!* that we just deleted

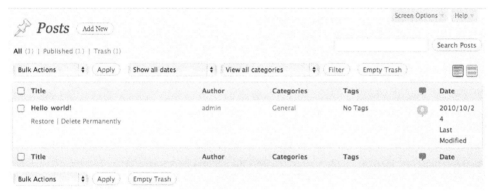

Figure 2.15 The Hello world! post in the Trash area

When we hover the mouse over the *Hello world!* post title in the trash management screen, two links will appear: *Restore* and *Delete Permanently*. If the *Restore* link is selected, the post will be restored, that is, it will again appear on our blog. If *Delete Permanently* link is selected, the post will be removed forever. We can also remove all the posts from the trash by selecting the *Empty Trash* button. We will select *Delete Permanently* to delete the *Hello world!* post forever.

2.8 Uploading Media

Besides text, we can insert media—images, videos, audios, and files—using the four icons located next to *Upload/Insert* text (see Figure 2.8). The icons represent Add *Image*, *Add Video*, *Add Audio*, and *Add Media*. Clicking any of these icons will bring up a Thickbox overlay window, which will allow us upload and insert media into the posts or pages.

Let's insert an image to our post. Select the *Add Image* icon located next to *Upload/Insert* text. A thickbox overlay window, shown in Figure 2.9, appears.

By default, WordPress opens a media uploader for adding media files to our site. The media uploader is based on Adobe Flash. If you have difficulty using the Flash uploader, you can use the *Browser uploader* link that opens a non-Flash version.

Note: We can upload multiple images with the Flash uploader.

The thickbox overlay window displays three tabs: *From Computer, From URL, and Media Library*:

- **From Computer**—Used for uploading the images from our local disk drive.

- **From URL**—Used for uploading the images from the Web.

- **Media Library**—Displays the images in the Media Library that we have already uploaded to our blog. We can insert any of these images from the Media Library into our posts or pages.

2.8.1 From Computer

When you select this option, you'll see a window with a *Select Files* button. When clicked, we'll see a dialog box that helps choose one or more images from a local drive. After selecting the image(s) that we want to upload, select the *Open* button and the images will be uploaded from our computer to the web server. For each file that's uploaded, we'll see a thumbnail image, along with the file name, file type, uploading date and dimensions, as shown in Figure 2.10. WordPress also prompts us to specify few image options. The fields shown in Figure 2.10 are explained in Table 2.2.

Table 2.2. Add Media Page Fields

Field	Usage
Edit Image	Opens up the basic image editor, included in the media uploader. The image editor allows us to resize, crop and rotate the uploaded image. Selecting the Edit Image button opens the image in the image editor, as shown in Figure 2.16.
Title	Used to enter the image title.
Alternate Text	Used to enter text related to the image displayed in the browser when the image doesn't load properly .This text is basically for visually impaired visitors. The text is read aloud when browsed with a screen reader.
Caption	Used to enter the image caption that appears underneath the image.
Description	Used to enter a brief description of the image.
Link URL	Used to enter the URL that we want to link with the image. There are three options that help decide the clickable status of the image. The three options are: **None**: makes the image non clickable. **File URL**: points to a file that displays detailed information or an enlarged size of the uploaded image **Post URL**: points to another post that is related to the current post or uploaded image.
Alignment	Used to align the image. There are four options to choose from: *Left, Center, Right,* or *None*.

Field	Usage
Size	Used to select the image size. The four options are: *Thumbnail, Medium, Large*, or *Full Size*. WordPress automatically creates small and medium-size versions of the uploaded images. A thumbnail is a smaller version of the original file. To specify or modify the size of the thumbnail, select the *Settings->Miscellaneous* option. In the *Image Sizes* section, specify the desired height and width of the small and medium thumbnail images generated by WordPress.
Insert into Post button	Used to insert the uploaded image into the post.
Save all changes	Used to insert a gallery of images into the post.

2.8.2 Editing Image

When an image is uploaded via the media uploader, a thumbnail of the uploaded image, plus file name, file type, date of uploading, and dimensions, are displayed, as shown in Figure 2.10. Below the thumbnail of the image is an *Edit Image* button, which opens an online image editor, as shown in Figure 2.16.

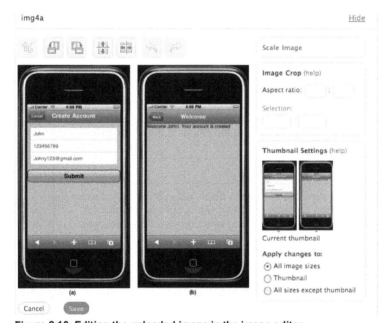

Figure 2.16. Editing the uploaded image in the image editor

The icons at the top are *Crop, Rotate counter-clockwise, Rotate clockwise, Flip vertically, Flip horizontally, Undo,* and *Redo* respectively:

- **Crop**—Crops the image
- **Rotate Counter-clockwise**—Rotates the image 90^0 counter-clockwise
- **Rotate clockwise**—Rotates the image 90^0 clockwise
- **Flip vertically**—Flips the image upside-down
- **Flip horizontally**—Mirrors the image

- **Undo**—Undoes the last action
- **Redo**—Repeats the last action

2.8.3 Cropping and Scaling Image

To crop the image, we click and drag a rectangle on the image. The region inside the rectangle is highlighted, as shown in Figure 2.17.

Figure 2.17. The highlighted region represents the region selected for cropping

The width and height of the area inside the rectangle is expressed as pixels in the Selection box. We can also precisely enter the width and height of the image in the Selection box, followed by clicking the Crop icon. The image will be cropped, as shown in Figure 2.18.

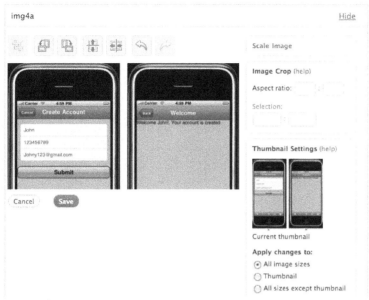

Figure 2.18. Cropped image

From the options available in *Apply changes to:*, we can determine whether we want the editing to be applied to all the images (*Thumbnail, Medium, Large* and *Full Size*), the thumbnail, or all the image sizes except the thumbnail. We can save the changes made to the image by clicking the *Save* button. Selecting *Cancel* will cancel all the editing applied to the image up to the last saved version.

Select the *Scale Image* link at the top right to scale the image. We'll see a box to specify the new width and height, as shown in Figure 2.19. After entering the desired width and height, click the *Scale* button.

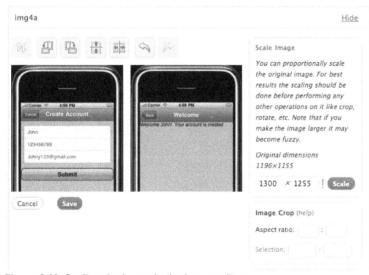

Figure 2.19. Scaling the image in the image editor

2.8.4 Adding Image Galleries

If we want to simultaneously add several images to the post , we can insert them as a gallery rather than individually. To insert a gallery into a post, add a new post or open an existing post in edit mode. In the *post content box*, place the cursor at the location where we want to insert the gallery and select the *Add Image* icon to upload images. To insert images in the form of gallery, we don't select *Insert into Post* button after uploading an image (see Figure 2.10). Instead, choose the *Save all changes* button to save the uploaded image. The image is saved as a part of an image gallery and consequently, a new tab, *Gallery (1)* appears at the top, along with the three tabs: *From Computer, From URL* and *Media Library*. The value (1) indicates that there is one image selected in the gallery. This number will increase when more images are uploaded. After uploading three images, for example *img4a.jpg, img5a.jpg* and *img1a.jpg*, the *Gallery* tab will display the thumbnails of all the images, along with their file names, as shown in Figure 2.20. The dialog box also prompts us to specify certain Gallery Settings.

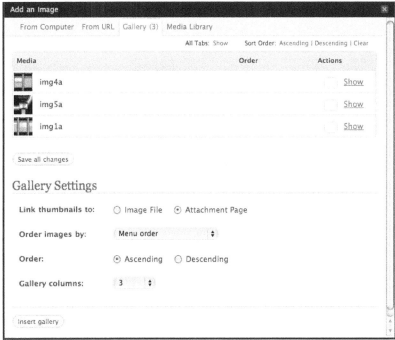

Figure 2.20. Gallery Settings dialog box

The value *(3)* in the *Gallery* tab tells us that three images are uploaded and can be inserted into a post in the form of a gallery. The thumbnail images appear in the order that they were uploaded (see Figure 2.20). We can change this sequence by specifying the order in the boxes below the *Order column*. For example, if we want the thumbnail of the images to begin with *img5a* followed by *img4a* image and finally the *img1a* image, we would enter 2,1, and 3 in the *Order* column, as shown in Figure 2.21.

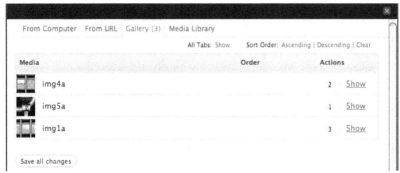

Figure 2.21. Modifying the order sequence of the gallery images

After entering the order sequence of the three images in the Order column, we can save the order by selecting the Save all changes button.

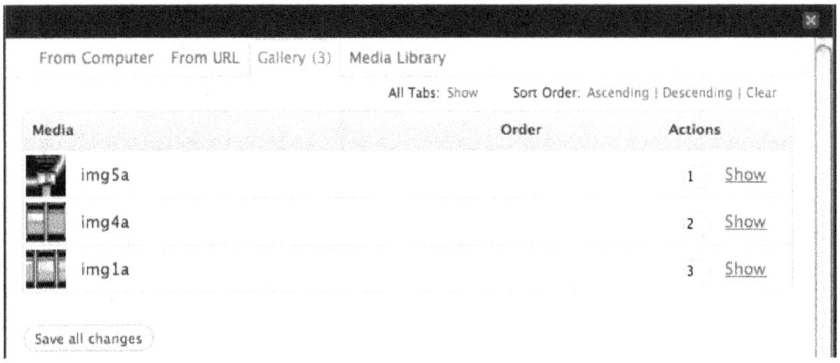

Figure 2.22. Gallery images with modified order sequence

The *Show* link under the *Actions* column displays the image settings of the selected image, as shown in Figure 2.10. We can change the image settings of the selected image, as well as insert the image into the post by selecting *Insert into Post button*. The *Save all changes* button is used for saving the changes that we may have made in any of the images. Under *Gallery Settings*, we find the following options:

- **Link Thumbnails To**: This setting asks where the thumbnails should jump to if the visitor clicks on the image. The setting provides two options: *Image File* and *Attachment Page*. The *Image File* option is the default and will show the image in the upper-left corner in the actual size it was uploaded. The *Attachment Page,* if supported by the current theme, will display the image in the center of the gallery along with thumbnails of the previous and next gallery images. If the current theme doesn't have an attachment page, the image will be displayed alone as if it were a single post.

- **Order Images By**: The drop-down menu allows us to set the order sequence of the images in the gallery based on any of the following three options: *Menu Order, Name*, and *Date/Time*. The *Menu Order* refers to the default order in which the images appear in the Gallery tab. The *Name* option is used to arrange the images on their file names and the *Date/Time* option is for arranging the images on the date and time of uploading

- **Order:** This setting lets you select either an Ascending or Descending order of the arrangement chosen in *Order Images By* drop-down menu

- **Gallery Columns**: This setting lets you select the number of columns for displaying the gallery of thumbnail images. Valid options are from 2 to 9.

- **Insert gallery button**—When this button is selected, WordPress inserts the gallery of images into our post. In HTML view, you'll see the following code, which designates that gallery is inserted:

```
[gallery]
```

After inserting the image gallery, it can be edited by selecting the *Edit Gallery* icon that appears in *Visual* view, marked by an ellipse in the Figure 2.23.

Figure 2.23. Edit Gallery icon in Visual view for editing the gallery settings

The image gallery in ascending order will appear in the post, as shown in Figure 2.24. We can see that the gallery displays the thumbnail size for each gallery image. We can change the thumbnail dimensions by selecting the *Media->Settings* option, as explained in detail in Chapter 7.

Figure 2.24. Image gallery, as seen on the blog

Let's now see how to upload images from the Web.

2.8.5 From URL

When the *From URL* tab, shown in Figure 2.9 is selected, we'll see the following page:

Figure 2.25. Media uploader dialog box for adding media from the Web

The fields displayed in Figure 2.25 are as follows:

- **Image URL**—Enter the full URL of the image that we want to add to our post. To find the URL of any image on the Web, right-click on it and select the *Properties* option from the pop-up menu.

- **Image Title**—Enter the title of the image in this box.

- **Alternate Text**—Enter a small description of the image to be displayed in the browser when the image doesn't load properly.

- **Image Caption**—Enter the image caption, which will appear underneath the image on our website.

- **Alignment**—Select any of the four options, *None*, *Left*, *Center* and *Right* to align the image in the post.

- **Link Image To**:—Enter the URL to which you want to link the image. When the image is clicked, a visitor will be navigated to the specified URL. There are two button below the text box:

    - **None:** Select this button if you don't want the image to be clickable.

    - **Link to Image**: Select this button to make the image clickable.

- **Insert into Post**—Inserts the image, whose URL we specified in the Image URL box, into the post.

2.8.6 Media Library

The images we uploaded to our blog get collected into a Media Library. These images can be inserted into blog posts at any time.

When the *Media Library* tab is selected, we'll see a page showing thumbnails of all the media uploaded to our server. The media files include Microsoft PowerPoint presentation files (.ppt), Microsoft Word documents (.doc), and Adobe Portable Document Format (.pdf) files. These file types can also contain images, video, and audio files. An example of a media library is shown in Figure 2.26.

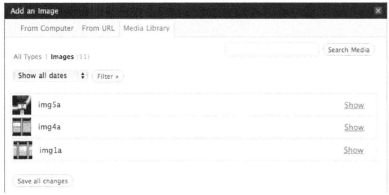

Figure 2.26. Images present in the Media Library

To insert any of the listed images into the post or to change image properties, select the *Show* link on the right of the image. A dialog box opens that displays all the properties associated with that image, as shown in Figure 2.27.

Figure 2.27. Displaying image properties of the selected image in the Media Library

From the dialog box, we can:

- Modify the properties of the image, such as image title, alternate text, caption, and image description

- Set the link URL of the image to link the image with another file or post.

- Align the image and select a size

- Select *Insert into Post* button to insert the selected image into the post

2.9 Adding Video

Adding a video to a post is very easy in WordPress. Here's how:

1. Add a new post to our blog or open an existing post in edit mode.

2. In the post content box, place the cursor at the location where we want to insert the video and select the Add Video icon next to the Upload/Insert text (see Figure 2.8).

3. The media uploader opens up in a thickbox overlay window, as shown in Figure 2.28. To upload video from the Web, select the *From URL* tab from the media uploader.

Figure 2.28. Specifying the URL and Title for the video to be uploaded

4. In the Video URL field, type the URL of the video file we want to use. The URL must be complete and include *http* and *www*.

5. In the Title field, type the title of the video so visitors can see the video subject. The title will appear in the form of link that the visitor may click to watch the video. Let's enter the title as *Old Friends*.

6. Finally, select the *Insert into Post* button.

7. Select the *Update* button to save all the changes made in the post.

Note: WordPress doesn't embed the actual video in the post; instead, it just inserts a link to the video. The visitors can click the link to load another page where the video will be played.

In the post, there is now a link, *Old Friends*, which, when selected, will take us to the source website and the video is played. Several video providers, including *YouTube,* provide video-embedding code that we can copy and paste into the post in *HTML* view. When you embed such code, we don't navigate to the source site; instead, the video will be played in directly in the post. We'll see an image of the video with a Play button in the center, as shown in Figure 2.29. Users can click the Play button to watch the video.

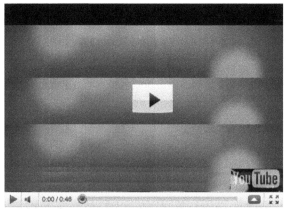

Figure 2.29. Video auto-embedded in a post

2.9.1 Auto-Embed feature

WordPress has an auto-embed feature for videos. If we type the video URL in plain text into the post body , WordPress automatically detects the URL and wraps the correct HTML embed code around that URL to make sure the video player displays in the post. For example, if we write URL of any YouTube video in plain text in the body of our post, WordPress will detect the URL and display the video player in our post, as shown in Figure 2.29. We can play the video in our post without having to navigate to the source site. To turn On the auto-embedding feature, check the *Attempt to automatically embed all plain text URLs* checkbox in the *Media Settings* dialog box, as shown in Figure 2.30.

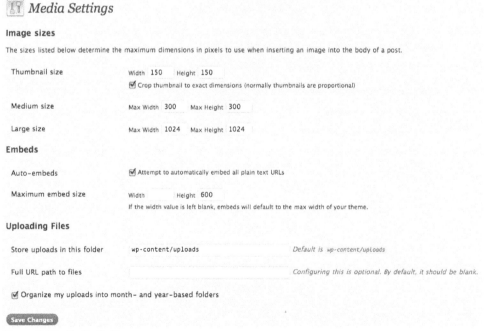

Figure 2.30. Media Settings page

Note: Media Settings are explained in detail in Chapter 7.

2.10 Adding Audio

WordPress does not have a built-in audio player, hence the uploaded video's audio track may not automatically embed in our post. To embed audio in our post, we need to install plug-in that support the desired audio format. There are many plug-in to choose from. I have chosen *WPaudio MP3 Player,* because it's easy to install, simple to use, is compatible with WordPress 3.0.3, and automatically converts the mp3 link into a player.

Note: The steps to search, install, and activate plugins are explained in detail in Chapter 6.

After installing and activating the *WPaudio MP3 Player,* we are ready to add audio to our post through the following steps :

1. Add a new post to our blog or open an existing post in edit mode.

2. In the *post content box,* place the cursor at the location where we want to insert the audio and select the *Add Audio* icon next to the *Upload/Insert* text (see Figure 2.8).

3. When the *Add Audio* icon is selected, the media uploader opens up in a thickbox overlay window, as shown in Figure 2.9. There are three tabs to insert audio:

   • **From Computer**—Uploads audio from the local disk drive

   • **From URL**—Specifies the URL link of the audio

   • **From Media Library**—Insert the audio from files already uploaded to the server

   If we have an audio on our local disk drive called *chaltechaltesong.mp3,* and select the *From Computer* tab in the media uploader box, the file will be uploaded to the following location on the server:

   `http://domain/wp-content/upload/year/month`

   That is, if the domain name is *example.com,* the current year is *2010* and the month is *October,* then the media file will be uploaded to the following location:

   `http://example.com/wp-content/uploads/2010/10`

   Note: The location of the uploaded media can be modified through *Uploading Files* section of Media Settings

   Select *Save all changes* button and close the media uploader window.

4. In the body of the post, write the command to access and play the audio file. The syntax for accessing and playing the audio file through *WPaudio MP3 Player* is:

   Syntax:

   ```
   [wpaudio url="Audio URL" class="wpaudio" autoplay="1" text="text to
   appear" dl="0"]
   ```

   where

   • **Audio URL** is the URL of the audio

   • **class="wpaudio"** converts the specified mp3 link into a player. To convert all post mp3 links into the player, select the *Settings->WPaudio* option from the main navigation menu and select the first option, *Convert all mp3 links.*

   • **autoplay="1"** is the attribute for autoplay

   • **text to appear** is the text that will appear on the post with the player

   • **dl="0"** disables downloads

Hence, using the above syntax, the command to access and play the audio file, chaltechaltesong.mp3 is:

```
[wpaudio url="http://example.com/wp-
content/uploads/2010/10/chaltechaltesong.mp3" class="wpaudio"
autoplay="1" text="Chalte Chalte" dl="0"]
```

The text that will appear on the post representing the audio is *Chalte Chalte*—the name of the song.

5. Select the *Update* button to save all the changes.

The post will show the audio player with the text Chalte Chalte, as shown in Figure 2.31. The player will autoplay when the post is loaded.

Figure 2.31. Audio Player playing the audio in a post

2.11 Pages

Unlike dynamic posts that change continuously, Pages are used for displaying static information. For example, the data specified in About Us or Contact Us is static and doesn't change often, and hence is displayed as pages. The ID, author, date, publication status, and page visibility will be set automatically when a page is published. The other difference between posts and pages is that, unlike posts, pages are organized into hierarchies, not by date. Thus, page(s) can be made "children" of other pages. Categories and tags are not available for pages. To manage blog pages, select Pages from the main navigation menu. A submenu will appear, as shown in Figure 2.32

Figure 2.32. Page menu options

When the *Pages* option is selected, the page management screen will open, displaying all existing blog pages in tabular format, as shown in Figure 2.33. We currently have only one page in page management screen—the default *About* page provided by WordPress. Managing pages in WordPress is similar to managing posts. We can search for pages with specific keywords by using the *Search* box on the top right. We can filter pages by selecting links such as *All, Published, Draft* and *Trash*. The *Show all dates* drop-down is used to list pages that were published on the desired date. To edit or delete several pages simultaneously, use the *Bulk Actions* drop-down menu and select the *Apply* button to execute the action.

Figure 2.33. Page Management screen

When the mouse is hovered over the *About* page, four links will appear: *Edit, Quick Edit, Trash,* and *View.*

- **Edit**—Opens the selected page in edit mode.

- **Quick Edit**—Though we cannot edit the contents of the page, still, we can edit several properties of the page with *Quick Edit* link, as shown in Figure 2.34.

Figure 2.34. Quick Edit screen for the About page

- We can change the *Parent* of the page if the page is not independent, but part of a main page.

- We can set the order sequence of the pages in which they will appear in the blog. To set the page sort order, enter a number in the *Order* field. For example, to make the page appear first in the blog, we enter value 0 in the Order field. Similarly, to make another page appear after the first page, set the order field to 1.

- The template is used to set the layout and appearance of the page. WordPress provides us with a *Default Template,* but we can create custom templates, as well.

- If the *Allow Comments* checkbox is checked, visitors may write comments about the page.

- The *Status* drop-down menu is used to edit the page status. The available options are *Pending Review, Draft,* and *Published.*

- The password field is used to make the page *password protected*, so only the visitors who know the password will be able to view the page. We just need to enter a password in the field and select the *Update* button to save the changes. Any visitor trying to access the page will be prompted to enter password, as shown in Figure 2.35.

Protected: About

This post is password protected. To view it please enter your password below:

Password:

(Submit)

Figure 2.35. Prompting the visitors for password when accessing a password-protected page

If we want the page to be accessed only by the admin, check the *Private* checkbox. Visitors will see *page not found* message, as shown in Figure 2.36.

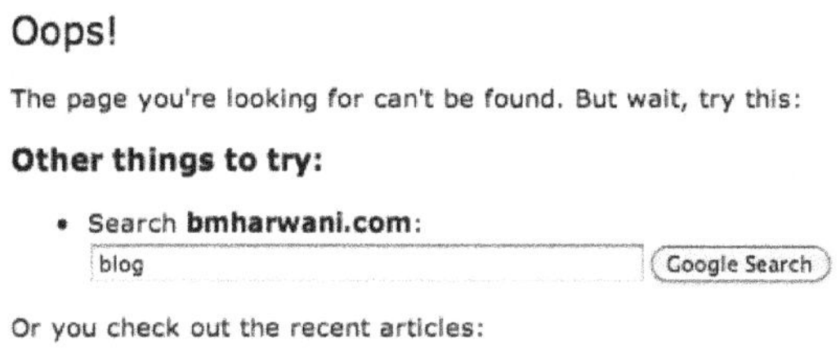

Oops!

The page you're looking for can't be found. But wait, try this:

Other things to try:

- Search **bmharwani.com**:

  | blog | | Google Search |

Or you check out the recent articles:

Figure 2.36. Error message while accessing a private page

When the administrator accesses a private page, he or she will see a *Private:* prefix on the page title.

- **Trash**—Used to delete the page. The page will reside in Trash area and can be restored or deleted permanently at any time.

- **View**—Displays the page as it will appear to a visitor.

2.11.1 Adding Page

Adding a page to the blog can be done in two ways: by clicking the *Pages->Add New* button from the main navigation menu or by selecting the Add New button from the page management screen. The resulting screen is shown in Figure 2.37.

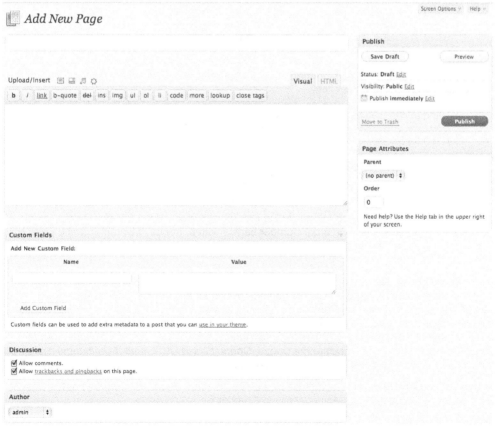

Figure 2.37. Add New Page screen

The fields shown in Figure 2.37 are explained in Table 2.3.

Table 2.3. Add New Page Fields

Field	Usage
Title box	Used to enter title of the page.
Page Content box	Used to enter page content.
Custom Fields	Used to add the custom fields that provide extra page information.
Discussion	Used to allow comments, pingbacks, and trackbacks for the page. By default, the "Allow Comments" and "Allow trackbacks and pingbacks on this page" checkboxes are selected. Uncheck them to disallow these options
Author	Used to choose the page author from the drop-down list.
Publish box	Used to change the state, visibility and publication date of the page.
Save Draft	Used to save the page in draft status. Draft status means that the page remains unpublished so we can word on it later.
Preview	Used to show the page as it will appear to the visitor when published.
Status	Used to change the page status to Published, Pending Review, or Draft.
Visibility	Used to set the visibility status of the page. The options are Public, Password Protected post, or Private.
Publish	Use to publish the page immediately or at another time. Select the Edit link to publish at the specified date and time.
Publish button	Used to display the page on the website.
Move to Trash	Used to delete the current page.
Page Attributes	Used to specify the page parent order sequence. This feature has two options: • Parent—Used to make the current page a sub-page of another page. From the drop-down list, select the page that will act as parent of the current page. • Order—Used to specify the order in which you want this page to appear on your site. The order number begins with 0, hence, if we enter 2, the page will appear as third page.

Pages can be organized into pages and *sub-pages*. A Page can have several sub-pages hence creating a hierarchy of pages. Let us assume that our organization has branches all over the world with its main office in Unites States. In that case, we create a Contact Us page displaying contact information of United States office. Also, we will create a series of pages displaying contact information of branches in other countries like UK, India, and China etc. These pages displaying information of the branches will be considered as sub pages of the main Contact Us page. To declare the pages, *Contact Us in UK, Contact Us in India* etc. as the sub-pages of the main Contact Us page, their *Parent* option must be set to *Contact Us* page

We will not be adding a new page to our blog right now, but we will show you how to edit the default *About* page. We will be adding a *Contact Us* page to our blog in Chapter 6.

2.11.2 Editing Page

To edit the *About* page, either select it from the *page management screen* or hover the mouse over the page title and choose the *Edit* link from the list that appears below the page title. The *About* page will open in edit mode, as shown in Figure 2.38.

Figure 2.38. Screen for editing the About page

Here, we see the default content provided by WordPress in the *About* page. Let's modify the page content by entering some text in the *page content* box. We don't need to edit the *Status, Visibility, Published,* or *Order* properties. After modifying the page content, save it by selecting the *Update* button. The edited About page appears in Figure 2.39.

bmharwani.com

bintu blog site

About

B.M. Harwani
Developer, Writer, and Entrepenuer

Areas of Expertise :

- .NET
- C#
- Java
- Joomla
- JQuery
- JSF
- JSP
- Objective C
- PHP
- VB

BIOGRAPHY

B.M.Harwani is founder and owner of Microchip Computer Education (MCE), based in
Ajmer, India that provides computer education in all programming and web developing
platforms. He graduated with a BE in computer engineering from the of Pune

Recent Posts
- Working with Forms

Recent Comments

Archives
- October 2010

Categories
- Smartphone Articles

Meta
- Site Admin
- Log out
- Entries RSS
- Comments RSS
- WordPress.org

Figure 2.39. Modified About page

Note: We will learn how to make a page the front page of the blog through Settings menu discussed
in Chapter 7

2.12 Post Tags

Tags are keywords that describe our post. They help the visitor to search for posts tagged with the desired
keywords. We create new tags by typing them into the *Tag* box in the *Post Tags* tab (see Figure 2.8). After
adding new tags, press *Add* button to apply them to the selected post. To manage tags, select *Post Tags*
from the *main navigation menu*. We will see the page shown in Figure 2.40. The left side of the page, is
used to add new tags to the blog and the right side, the *post tags management screen,* is used for creating,
editing, and deleting post tags in our blog.

Figure 2.40. Post Tags screen

Adding a new tag to the blog is very simple. All we need is to fill in the *Name, Slug,* and *Description* fields that appear on the left side of the page and click the *Add New Tag* button. Editing the tags is also very easy. We either select the tag name from *the post tags management screen* or hover the mouse over the tag name and select the *Edit* link that appears below the tag name. The links that appear below the tag name are:

- **Edit**—Opens the Post Tags edit page allowing us to edit the name, slug, and description of the tag
- **Quick Edit**—Allows editing of the tag's name and slug
- **Delete**—Sends the selected tag to trash

After making the desired modifications, save the tag by selecting *Update* button.

2.13 Summary

In this chapter, we learned how to add content to our blog in the form of posts and pages. We also saw how to create and manage categories and assign the post to different categories. We learned how to upload media—images, videos, and audio—to our post. Next, we will learn to make the blog dynamic by adding themes. We will also learn how to increase functionality of our blog by installing and activating plugins.

3

Managing Media, Links and Comments

In the previous chapter, we learned how to add content to our blog through posts and pages. We also learned to manage categories and assign posts to different categories. Finally, we learned to upload media, i.e., images, videos and audios to posts and pages of our blog. In this chapter, we will learn to manage three aspects of our blog, namely, *Media Library*, *Links* and *Comments*. Let us have a brief idea of each of these aspects:

- **Media** as we know includes images, audio, video and other files. Recall from the previous chapter that we have already learned to add media to the Media Library while inserting it into a post or a page. That is, we learned to add media to the library that was associated with any post or page. In this chapter, we will learn to add, delete and manage media to the Media Library directly which can then be inserted into posts or pages whenever desired.

- **Links** as we know are the popular means for navigation. In this chapter, we will learn to create a new link category, manage links in the link category and understand links of the Blogroll (a default link category provided by the WordPress).

- **Comments** are the responses of the visitors on the posts published on our blog. In this chapter, we will learn the process of moderating comments that is, how to delete comments, mark them as spam, edit and approve them.

Let us now begin this chapter with Media Management.

3.1 Managing Media Library

All the media files present in our blog, i.e., images, video, audio, and other files can be seen and managed through the Media Library. To open the Media Library, select the Media option from the main navigation menu. The sub menu options of the Media menu are shown in Figure 3.1.

Figure 3.1 Options of the Media menu

Now select the *Library* option from the Media menu. The *Media Library* page opens up as shown in Figure 3.2. This page helps manage, add or delete the media files that are currently present in our blog. Note that media uploaded using WordPress only will be displayed on this page. That is, any media uploaded through FTP will not be displayed.

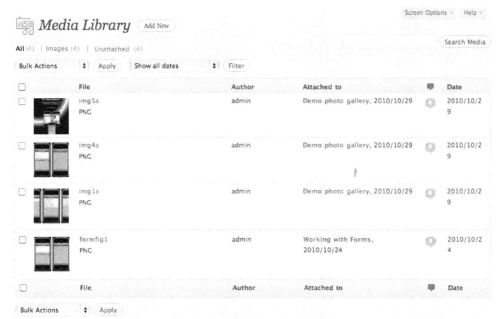

Figure 3.2 List of media on the Media Library page

Figure 3.2 shows four image files that we had uploaded while creating the post, *Working with Forms* and image gallery in Chapter 2. We can filter media using the filter links, namely, *All, Images* and *Unattached* located at the top of the page. *All* link displays all media files, audio, video, images, pdf, etc. whether attached to any post/page or directly uploaded to the Media Library. The *Images* link displays all the images whether attached or not to some posts or pages. The *Unattached* link displays all the media that are not attached to any post or page. Recall that media can be uploaded to our blog in two ways, either by inserting the media into the post or page or directly adding it into the Media Library. The media that are directly added to the Media Library are known as *unattached media*.

When we select the *Unattached* link, a new button appears, *Scan for Lost Attachments,* besides the *Apply* button. The *Scan for Lost Attachments* button checks the database for any unattached images. On hovering on any unattached image, a link appears to *attach* that image. This link when selected opens a thickbox overlay window that searches the desired post or page to which we want to attach the image.

We can also search our media using the search box at the top right-hand side of the Media Library page. When the media is uploaded while inserting it into a post or a page, the *Attached to* column displays the *title* and *date* of the post or page on which the media is attached. The *Attached to* column appears as blank for a media that is uploaded directly using the Media Library window.

Through the *Bulk Actions* drop down menu, we can delete media in bulk. There are two ways to do this, first select the checkbox to the left of the media that you want to delete. Second, select the checkbox at the top to auto select them all and then select the *Delete* option from the *Bulk Actions* drop-down menu.

Note: Do not forget to select the *Apply* button after selecting an action from the Bulk Actions drop down menu.

On hovering the mouse over any media in the Media Library page, we are presented with three links, *Edit, Delete Permanently* and *View*. Selecting the *Delete Permanently* link deletes the selected media whereas selecting the *View* link displays the selected media on the blog. For example, selecting the *View* link on the image *formfig1* displays it on the blog as shown in Figure 3.3.

bmharwani.com

bintu blog site

Home   About

formfig1

By admin | Published October 24, 2010 | Full size is 447 × 432 pixels | Edit

(a)   (b)

Recent Posts
- Working with Forms

Recent Comments

Archives
- October 2010

Categories
- Smartphone Articles

Meta
- Site Admin
- Log out
- Entries RSS
- Comments RSS
- WordPress.org

Figure 3.3 Viewing form1fig1 image on the blog

Selecting the *Edit* link will open the media in edit mode.

3.1.1 Editing Media

To edit a media, hover the mouse over it in the Media Library page, and select the *Edit* link that appears below the media name. Selecting the *Edit* link will open the media in the edit mode. For example, selecting the *Edit* link on the image, *img5a.png* opens it in the edit mode as shown in Figure 3.4.

Figure 3.4 Editing the image img5a.png

We can add and edit *Title, Alternate Text, Caption* and *Description* of the image. After making the desired modifications, we select the *Update Media* button to save all the changes.

3.1.2 Uploading Media

We can upload media to our WordPress blog by either selecting the *Add New* menu item from the Media menu or by selecting the *Add New* button from the Media Library window. The screen for uploading new media is shown in Figure 3.5.

Figure 3.5 Screen for uploading new media

Through this screen, we can add files to the Media Library directly without associating it with any post or page. This media can be later inserted into posts and pages whenever desired. We use the *Select Files* button to upload media using the Flash-based media uploader. In case of any problem using the Flash based media uploader, we can select the *Browser Uploader* link to open the browser uploader.

Note: The browser uploader can upload only a single file at a time. Whereas, with Flash based media uploader, we can upload multiple files. We just need to select a group of files in the dialog box followed by selecting the Open button.

After getting hold of all the options of the Media Library, let us go ahead and understand how the Link categories and links are managed.

3.2 Managing Links

Links are the means to connect our blog to another blog, website, post, page, image, etc. The links can be internal or external. The internal links navigate us to the content that already exists in our blog whereas external links navigate us to the content that is external to our blog. In this section, we will learn to manage links as well as link categories. To manage links of our blog, we select the *Links* menu from the main navigation menu. The menu items of the Links menu appear as shown in Figure 3.6.

Figure 3.6 Options of the Links menu

On selecting the *Links* menu item, we get a screen known as the *links management screen* that is used for managing links as shown in Figure 3.7. The links that we see are the links of the default link category known as *Blogroll*. When we add new link categories, as we will see later, we can filter to see the links of the desired link category by choosing it from the *View all Categories* drop down menu next to the *Apply* button. The *View all Categories* drop down menu at the moment shows only two options, View *All Categories* and *Blogroll*. However, as we add new link categories, they would also appear in this drop down menu. By default, links displayed are arranged in the order of their names as declared by the *Order by Name* drop down menu. The *Order by Name* drop down menu displays four options, *Order by Link ID, Order by Name, Order by Address* and *Order by Rating* to sort the links on the basis of their IDs, name, address or rating, respectively. While creating links, we will learn to rate by assigning it a value between 0 and 10 to represent its importance, usefulness or popularity.

The *Blogroll* is a default link category provided to us by the WordPress. These links point at the information about plugins, support, forums, themes, development, etc. being displayed on the wordpress.org site. On hovering over any link name, we are presented with two links, *Edit* and *Delete*. Selecting the *Edit* link opens the selected link in the edit mode whereas the *Delete* link moves the selected link to the trash. We can also use the *Bulk Actions* drop down menu present at the top of the page to edit or delete several links simultaneously. For example, to delete more than one link, all we need to do is to select the box to the left of the link name(s) followed by selecting the *Delete* option from the *Bulk Actions* drop down menu. After selecting an action from the *Bulk Actions* drop down menu, we select the *Apply* button to execute the action.

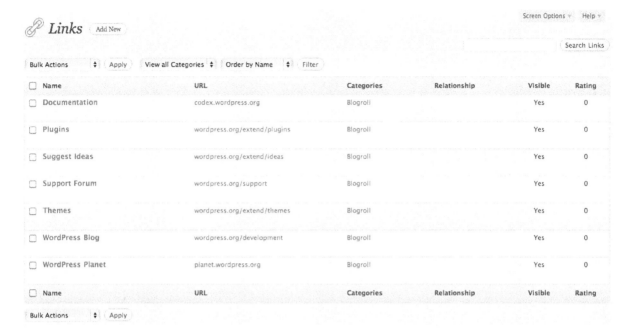

Figure 3.7 Links Management Screen

Since, every link has to be assigned to a link category, before adding a new link, let us first create a new link category.

3.2.1 Creating link categories

Link categories provide us a way of dividing our links into different categories, that is, we can keep related links together in one category. To add a new category, select *Links -> Link Categories* option from the main navigation menu. We get a screen to add a new link category as shown in Figure 3.8. The right-hand side of the screen is the *link categories management* area that displays the link categories that already exist in our blog. As expected, we find a link category, *Blogroll* — the default link category provided by the WordPress.

Figure 3.8 Page to add and manage link categories

Let us create a new link category by the name, *My Articles*. In this link category we add some links that point to some of my articles published on the other websites. The usage of the fields required in creating a new link category is as follows:

- **Link Category name**—Used to specify the name of the new link category. Let us enter the name of the new link category as *My Articles*.

- **Link Category slug**—Used to enter the URL friendly version of the link category name. If we leave this field blank, it is auto created by converting the link category name into lowercase and connecting each word with hyphens. For example, the Link Category slug for the link category named *My Articles* will be my-articles.

- **Description**—Used to enter a small description of the link category. Let us enter the description as, "This link category will contain the links of my published articles".

- **Add Category button**—Used to create a new link category.

After entering the information in the fields as discussed, when we select the *Add Category* button, the link category *My Articles* gets created and appears in the *link categories management* area on the right-hand side as shown in Figure 3.9.

Figure 3.9 Link Categories Management area showing the newly added link category, My Articles

On hovering the mouse over a link category name in the link categories management area three links appear below the link category name, *Edit, Quick Edit* and *Delete*. The *Edit* link allows us to modify all the three fields of the selected link category. That is, we can modify the Link Category Name, Link Category slug and Description of the selected link category. The *Quick Edit* link allows us to modify only two fields, the Link Category Name and Link Category slug of the selected link category. The *Delete* link permanently deletes the selected link.

Note: Deleting a link category does not delete the links in that category, but instead assigns all the links to the default category (Blogroll).

Now that we have created a new link category by name *My Articles*, let us add a few links to it.

3.2.2 Adding new links to the link category

To add a new link, either select *Links->Add New* option from the main navigation menu or select the *Add New* button from the *links management screen*. By either method, we get a screen to add a new link as shown in Figure 3.10.

Figure 3.10 Page for adding a new link

Assuming, I have an article titled, *Forward Navigation Via Toolbar Buttons* published on my website, `http://bmharwani.com`. Let us add a link to this article in our newly created link category, *My Articles*. The meaning of the fields used in adding a new link is explained in Table 3.1.

Table 3.1 Brief description of the fields of the Add new Link page

Field	Usage
Name	Enter the name of the website or web page that we want to link. In this case we add the title of the article that we want to link, that is, *Forward Navigation Via Toolbar Buttons*.
Web Address	Enter the URL of the website or web page to which we want to link. The URL has to be complete, i.e., we have to include *http://* part while entering the URL. Let us enter the URL of the article here as `http://bmharwani.com/ForwardNavigationToolbarbuttons.htm`
Description	Enter a small description of the target website. This description will be displayed on hovering the mouse over the link. Let us enter a small description as *"The article explains how to use the toolbar buttons for forward navigation through jQTouch."*
Categories	Select the checkbox of the category in which we want this new link to appear. We can view the *most used* link categories by selecting *Most Used* link, and can create new link categories by clicking the *+Add New Category* link. Since, we want our new link to appear in the new link category, *My Articles*, let us select the *My Articles* checkbox.
Target	The target determines the way we want this link to load on the visitor's browser window, i.e., whether the link should appear in the same window or in the new window. The available choices are • **_blank**: Loads the link in a new browser window. • **_top**: Loads the link in the top frame—applicable when our blog site is designed with frames. • **None:** Loads the link in the same browser window. This is the default choice. Let us select **_blank** option to make the linked article appear in the new browser window.
Link Relationship (XFN)	Allows us to select the option to specify our relationship with the person we are linking to. XFN stands for *XHTML Friends Network* and helps specify our relationship with the people we are linking to. • **Identity**: Check this checkbox if the link is for our own website. • **Friendship:** Check the checkbox, *Contact, Acquaintance, Friend* or *None* that identifies the relationship. • **Physical:** Check the checkbox if we have met the person we are linking to. • **Professional:** Check the checkbox, co-worker or colleague if the person we are linking to is a co-worker or a colleague. • **Geographical:** Check the checkbox, co-resident, neighbor or none to determine if the person we are linking lives with us, or is our neighbor or none of these. • **Family:** Check the checkbox to specify whether the person we are linking to

Field	Usage
	is a family member. Select the option, *child, kin, parent, sibling, spouse* or *none* that identifies how the person is related to us.
	• **Romantic:** Check the checkbox that specifies the type of romantic relationship we have with the person we are linking to. That is, whether we have a crush on him/her, or he/she is our muse, date or sweetheart.
	Since, the article to which I am going to link, belongs to my website, let us select the first checkbox, *Identity* that says *another web address of mine*. On selecting the *Identity* checkbox, we find that a word *me* automatically appears in the *rel:* field that expresses the relation of the link.
Advanced	Allows us to specify advanced settings given as follows:
	• **Image Address**: Enter the URL of the image of the link. Some WordPress themes display the image also along with the link. Assuming the image of the link is *linkimage.png* and it exists on the target website, let us enter the URL of the image as `http://bmharwani.com/linkimage.png`
	• **RSS Address:** Type the RSS feed URL of the blog we are linking to. WordPress displays the link to the site's RSS feed along with the link.
	• **Notes:** Enter some information about the link for our reference. This information will not be displayed on the blog and is meant for us only.
	• **Rating:** Select the Rating drop-down list to rate this link from 0 to 10, 0 being the worst and 10 being the best. Some WordPress themes display the links in the order in which they are rated, from best to worst.
Keep this link private	Select this checkbox if we do not want to display the link publicly on our blog.
Add Link	Select this button to save the link.

On selecting the *Add Link* button, the new link titled, *Forward Navigation Via Toolbar Buttons* will be added to our link category, *My Articles*. To display, the links and link categories on the blog, we need to take the help of *Links Widget* explained in the next chapter.

Let us go ahead and see how comments are managed on a blog.

3.3 Managing Comments

Comments are the views or feedback of the visitors on the posts published. To avoid spam and misuse of the comments, they are moderated by default before being published. In order to manage comments, we select the Comments icon (refer to Figure 3.11) from the main navigation menu.

Figure 3.11 Comments icon in the main navigation menu

On selecting the Comments icon from the main navigation menu, we get a *comments management screen* as shown in Figure 3.12. The screen is supposed to show all comments across our entire blog but since none of our posts is yet commented, no comment is displayed on the comment management screen.

💬 *Comments*

All | Pending (0) | Approved | Spam (0) | Trash (0)

Show all comment types ⬍   Filter

No comments found.

Figure 3.12 Comments Management Screen

Let us add a comment to a post to learn more.

3.3.1 Adding Comments

Let us assume that a visitor by name *bintu* comments on our post *Working with Forms* as shown in Figure 3.13.

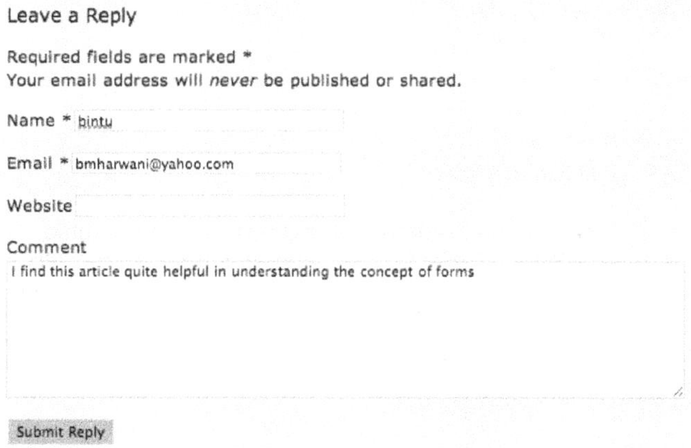

Leave a Reply

Required fields are marked *
Your email address will *never* be published or shared.

Name * bintu

Email * bmharwani@yahoo.com

Website

Comment
I find this article quite helpful in understanding the concept of forms

Submit Reply

Figure 3.13 Posting comment to the post, Working with Forms

The *Name* and *Email* are the required fields and cannot be left blank. The *Website* input field is optional. After entering the comment, visitor needs to select the *Submit Reply* button to post the comment. The comment will be received and the visitor is informed that the comment will be published after it is moderated.

3.3.2 Moderating Comments

To avoid comment spam, the WordPress by default requires that a commenter has a previously approved comment before posting. All new comments are automatically placed in moderation and will not be published until they are approved either through the *Comments* menu found on the main navigation menu or the *Recent Comments* box on the dashboard. We can change this setting through the *Settings-> Discussion* option (refer Figure 7.35). We can also force all comments to be placed in moderation, i.e., whether there is a previously approved comment or not, the comment will be published only after the administrator approves it.

Comment Spam

Comment spam refers to the comment that is unwanted and is meant for promoting another website or product. The *Settings->Discussion* option has multiple settings to reduce the amount of comment spam received by our blog. For example, we can hold a comment in the moderation queue if it contains more than two links. Multiple links in a comment is a common characteristic of a spam. WordPress also provides a *keyword blacklist* allowing us to automatically declare a comment as spam if it contains any of the specified keywords.

What happened to the comment that was written by the visitor *bintu* on our post, *Working with Forms*? Lets get back to it. An automatic email is sent to the author of the post informing that the post is commented. The content of the email may appear as shown in Figure 3.14. The author is provided links to email the commenter, see all the comments related to the specified post, move the comment to trash and to mark it as spam.

Figure 3.14 Email received by the post author when a post is commented

Also, an email is sent to the administrator to inform that a post is commented and has to be moderated. The content of the email may appear as shown in Figure 3.15. The email contains several links to help the administrator view the comment, send email to the commenter, approve the comment, move the comment to trash, mark it as a spam, etc.

Figure 3.15 Email received by the administrator when a post is commented

The *comments management screen* that was previously empty will now display the comment as shown in Figure 3.16. We can see that the comments are displayed along with the information of the commenter such as name, e-mail, IP address, etc. Comments can be filtered using the links at the top, *All, Pending, Approved, Spam* and *Trash*. We can also search comments for specific keywords using the search box located at the top right. The drop down menu besides the *Apply* button has an option selected by default, *Show all comment types*, which means comments as well as pings both be displayed. We can use this drop down menu to see only comments or only pings. Pings are different from comments as we will see in the section Trackbacks and Pings. On hovering the mouse over any comment, different moderation options will be displayed such as *Approve, Reply, Quick Edit, Edit, Spam* and *Trash*.

Figure 3.16 A comment displayed on the Comments Management Screen

On selecting the *Reply* link, we get a box to reply to the comment directly as shown in Figure 3.17.

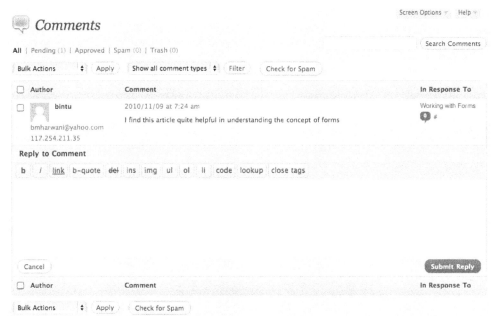

Figure 3.17 Box for replying to the comment

After writing the reply in the large text box, we need to select the *Submit Reply* button to send it to the commenter. The *Quick Edit* link allows us to edit the *Name, E-mail, URL* and comment text as shown in Figure 3.18. We cannot change the status of the comment through the *Quick Edit* link, i.e., we cannot approve the comment, move it to trash or mark it as a spam. After making the desired modifications, we need to select the *Update Comment* button to save the changes.

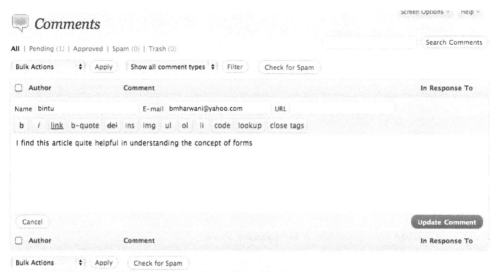

Figure 3.18 The Quick Edit screen for quick and small edits on the comment

The *Edit* link not only allows modifying the *Name, E-mail, URL* and comment text but also allows changing the status of the comment. The comment can be any of the given status, *Approved, Pending* or *Spam* as shown by the radio buttons in Figure 3.19. That is, we can approve a comment, keep it pending, declare it as a spam or move it to *Trash*. We need to select the *Update Comment* button to apply the modifications made.

Figure 3.19 A comment in the edit mode

On marking any comment as a spam, the *comments management screen* makes the comment invisible and informs that the comment of the specified commenter is marked as spam. Also a link *Undo* is displayed (refer to Figure 3.20) which when selected makes the comment visible again.

Figure 3.20 Marking the comment as spam

Similarly, on selecting the *Trash* link, the selected comment disappears from *the comment management screen* and is moved to trash. The screen also informs that the comment by the specified commenter is moved to trash along with an *Undo* link that can be used to get the comment back. Let us go ahead and approve the comment by selecting the *Approve* link. Once approved, the comment is displayed as a public comment as shown in Figure 3.21.

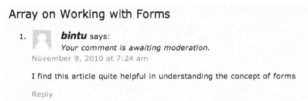

Figure 3.21 Comment displayed at the end of the post

In order to view all the comments for a given post, select the *comment* icon (marked in circle as shown in Figure 3.22) in the *post management screen*. The numerical value within the comment icon designates the number of approved comments on the post. Clicking the icon filters all comments and only displays comments for that particular post.

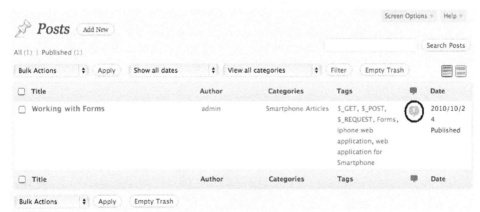

Figure 3.22 Comments icon in the Post Management Screen

3.3.3 Trackbacks and Pings

Trackback is a method for sending notification between websites. Usually the notifications or pings are sent from other sites when they link to any of our post or reversely when in our post we add a link to their post. When the post is published, our blog will ping or notify the linked blog informing that its content is linked in our post. The blog receiving the notification may approve, trash or spam the trackback exactly the way in

[67]

which the comments are dealt. The notification is sent via a network *ping*, a tool that is used to test, or verify, whether a link is reachable from our site to the linked site.

Trackbacks appear alongside comments on a post and is a popular technique to inform the readers that the current post is referred to or discussed elsewhere. It is also considered as a good way of knowing that other blogger(s) appreciate and like the information posted by us and vice versa.

Let us understand this concept with an example. Assume that there are two blogs with URLs `http://bmharwani.com` and `http://bintuharwani.wordpress.com` where the blog of the URL `http://bmharwani.com` belongs to us and the blog of the URL `http://bintuharwani.wordpress.com` belongs to some other blogger. Now if the blogger of `bintuharwani.com` adds a link to the post of our blog, *Working with Forms* in his new post titled, *Different methods of sending data from one PHP script to another* and the moment the blogger publishes this post, his/her blog pings our blog and consequently the administrator of our blog receives an email as shown in Figure 3.23. If we do not get a mail, it means the trackbacks is not enabled on our blog. To enable trackbacks, select the *Settings->Discussion* menu item from the main navigation menu and check the checkbox, *Allow link notifications from other blogs (pingbacks and trackbacks)*.

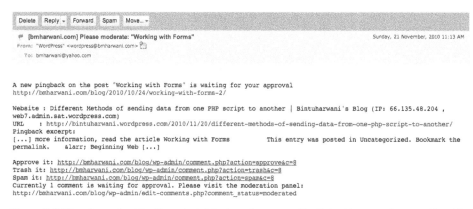

Figure 3.23 Email received by the administrator when a post is linked to a post on another blog

The email displays the information of the blogger such as its URL, IP address, the title of the post that is linked to our post etc. and will ask the administrator to either approve the pingback or mark it as a spam or send it to trash via different links. Let us go ahead and approve the pingback. Since, trackbacks are basically considered as remote comments on our post, the *Moderate Comment* page opens as shown in Figure 3.24 asking for confirmation.

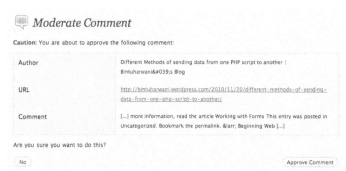

Figure 3.24 Moderate Comment page to approve or disapprove the pingback on our post

We can even change our mind to approve the pingback by selecting the *No* button. To approve the pingback, we need to select the *Approve Comment* button. When the pingback is approved, it will *appear* on the *comments management screen* as shown in Figure 3.25. Also, our blog will automatically send an email to the author of the post informing of the new pingback that is attached to his/her post.

Figure 3.25 Comments Management Screen showing the comments and pingbacks

In the blog, below the post, *Working with Forms*, a new comment appears containing link to the post that linked our post as shown in Figure 3.26.

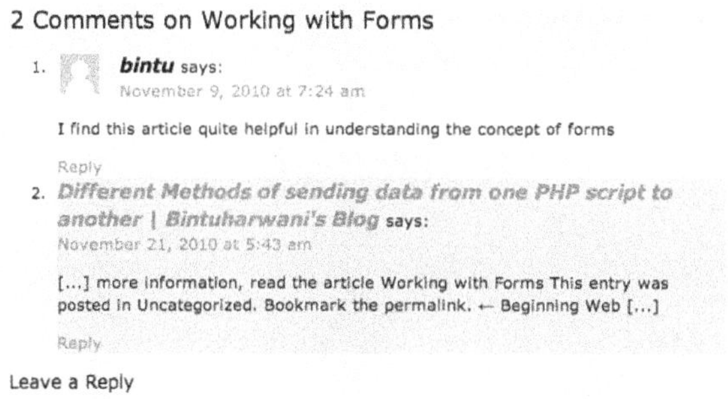

2 Comments on Working with Forms

1. **bintu** says:
   November 9, 2010 at 7:24 am

   I find this article quite helpful in understanding the concept of forms

   Reply

2. *Different Methods of sending data from one PHP script to another | Bintuharwani's Blog* says:
   November 21, 2010 at 5:43 am

   [...] more information, read the article Working with Forms This entry was posted in Uncategorized. Bookmark the permalink. ← Beginning Web [...]

   Reply

Leave a Reply

Figure 3.26 The approved pingback appears as a new comment

The comment displays the link to the post, *Different methods of sending data from one PHP script to another* that contains a link to our post. The reader of our post can select the link to view the remote post and can navigate back to our post through the link that is present in the remote post. The Trackback option therefore allows the reader to refer back and forth between the documents just like reciprocal linking.

So, it is clear that whenever we add a link to any post of another blog in our post, the remote blog will be notified about it whenever our post is published. We can also inform some other sites about the new post if needed. To do this, we just need to add the URLs of those sites to which we want to inform about the new post in the *Send Trackbacks to:* box while editing or adding a post. Besides this, the list of sites mentioned in the *Update Services* section of our *Writing Settings* will also be pinged (refer Chapter 7 for details).

Ping is an XML-RPC signal that will alert a server by saying there is a new or updated material on a particular website or blog. This signal informs the news aggregators that some changes have taken place to our blog and invites them to index all the changes. By default our blog pings an update service, such as *Ping-o-Matic*, to inform that a new post is published on our blog. The idea is to drive traffic to our blog.

To enable pinging URLs in the posts, make sure there is a check mark next to *"Attempt to notify any Weblogs linked to from the article"* in the *Settings->Discussion* menu item of the main navigation menu (refer Figure 7.35).

In case you do not find, *Send trackbacks to: box* in our post, open the *Screen Options* from the top right corner of the screen and check *the Send Trackbacks* checkbox as shown in Figure 3.27.

Figure 3.27 Screen options to display sections in the post

We can explicitly allow or block trackbacks and pings to a post using the checkbox *Allow trackbacks and pingbacks* found in the post as shown in Figure 3.28. This setting will override the options selected in the *Settings->Discussion* page.

Figure 3.28 Checkbox to control the trackbacks and pings on the post

You must have noticed that in the above discussion, we have mixed up the terms trackbacks and pingbacks. It is done as there is very less difference between the two. They have the same function but they use an entirely different protocol. A pingback is essentially an XML-RPC request sent from one blog to another. Pingback is less prone to spam than trackback because when a blog receives a pingback from another blog, it goes out and checks the originating blog for the existence of a live incoming link.

When the post is published, we can verify that pinging has taken place by opening the post in the edit mode. The *Send Trackbacks* section displays a list of the sites that have already been pinged. The following figure 3.29 mentions that it has already pinged `http://bintuharwani.wordpress.com`

Figure 3.29 Send Trackbacks section of the post displaying the URL that is already pinged

Trackbacks are often abused by SpamBots and may cause various problems hence it is better to disable this option. To do this, select the *Settings->Discussion* menu item from the main navigation menu and uncheck the checkbox, *Allow link notifications from other blogs (pingbacks and trackbacks)*.

3.4 Summary

In this chapter, we learned to manage the Media Library, i.e., how media is uploaded, edited and deleted. Next, we learned about the Links and Links Categories management. We also learned to create new link categories and add links to the link categories. Finally, we saw how comments are moderated in a blog and how comments are different from pings.

In the next chapter, we will learn to make our blog dynamic by applying new themes to it. We will also learn to add custom menus to the blog and make the frequently used contents of our blog quite accessible to the visitors by making it appear through widgets in the sidebars.

4

Making the Blog Dynamic

In the previous chapter, we learned to upload, edit and delete media through the Media Library. We also learned to manage link categories and understood how the links are managed inside them. Finally, we learned the process of comment moderation and the concept behind trackbacks and pings.

In this chapter, we will learn to:

- **Manage Themes**—Adding themes is the best way to make a blog appear attractive and dynamic. In this chapter, we will learn to search, install and activate and deactivate themes.

- **Manage Custom Menus**—Custom Menus are used at large for developing navigation, i.e., adding links and internal and external URLs to pages. In this chapter, we will learn to create, add and remove links from the custom menus.

- **Using Widgets**—Widgets are highly used for displaying required information on the sidebars. In this chapter, we will learn the usage of each of these widgets in detail and understand how each widget is configured to display the required information.

- **Knowing the theme editor**—We will understand the role of the theme editor in editing the selected theme.

Let us start our journey into the world of themes.

4.1 Themes

Themes are used for enhancing the look-and-feel of our blog. A theme provides attractive fonts, colors, graphics and content layout. Applying themes is the quickest way to make our blog appear dynamic. There are different types of themes available such as standard blog themes, corporate themes, photo themes, etc. To apply a theme, select the *Appearance* menu from the *main navigation menu*. On doing this, we get the submenu options as shown in Figure 4.1.

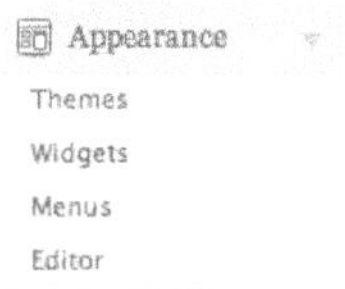

Figure 4.1 Menu options of the Appearance menu

On selecting the *Themes* option from the *Appearance* menu, we get a screen that has two tabs, *Manage Themes* and *Install Themes*.

4.1.1. Managing Themes

The *Manage Themes* tab is selected by default and lists all the themes that are currently installed on our server. The *Manage Themes* tab does the function of managing themes such as activating or deactivating any theme, upgrading a theme, etc. Figure 4.2 shows a single theme *Twenty Ten* that is installed by default on our server while installing WordPress. The themes that are installed on our server are placed in the *wp-content/themes* directory of the server. These themes are displayed along with a screenshot, a theme name, a link to the author's website and a short description of the theme.

Current Theme

Twenty Ten 1.0 by the WordPress team

The 2010 default theme for WordPress.

All of this theme's files are located in /themes/twentyten .

Tags: black, blue, white, two-columns, fixed-width, custom-header, custom-background, threaded-comments, sticky-post, translation-ready, microformats, rtl-language-support, editor-style

There is a new version of Twenty Ten available. View version 1.1 Details or upgrade automatically.

Available Themes

You only have one theme installed right now. Live a little! You can choose from over 1,000 free themes in the WordPress.org Theme Directory at any time: just click on the *Install Themes* tab above.

Figure 4.2 Manage Themes tab displaying the default theme, Twenty Ten

On clicking any of the listed themes, we can view its real-time preview. Let us now see how to install more themes on our blog.

4.1.2 Installing Themes

The *Install Themes* tab is for installing new themes on our server. On selecting the *Install Themes* tab, we get a search screen as shown in Figure 4.3. Here, we can search for themes by *keyword*, *author* or *tag*. We can also specify the list of the features such as the *color, columns, width, features* and *subject* of the theme that we are looking for by selecting on the appropriate checkboxes. After selecting the desired checkboxes, we select the *Find Themes* button to get the list of the themes that satisfy a given criteria. For example, to search for a theme that has *blue* color, *three columns* layout, has *flexible width, custom-background* and *custom-menu* and is of *seasonal* subject, we check the checkboxes as shown in Figure 4.3 followed by selecting the *Find Themes* button.

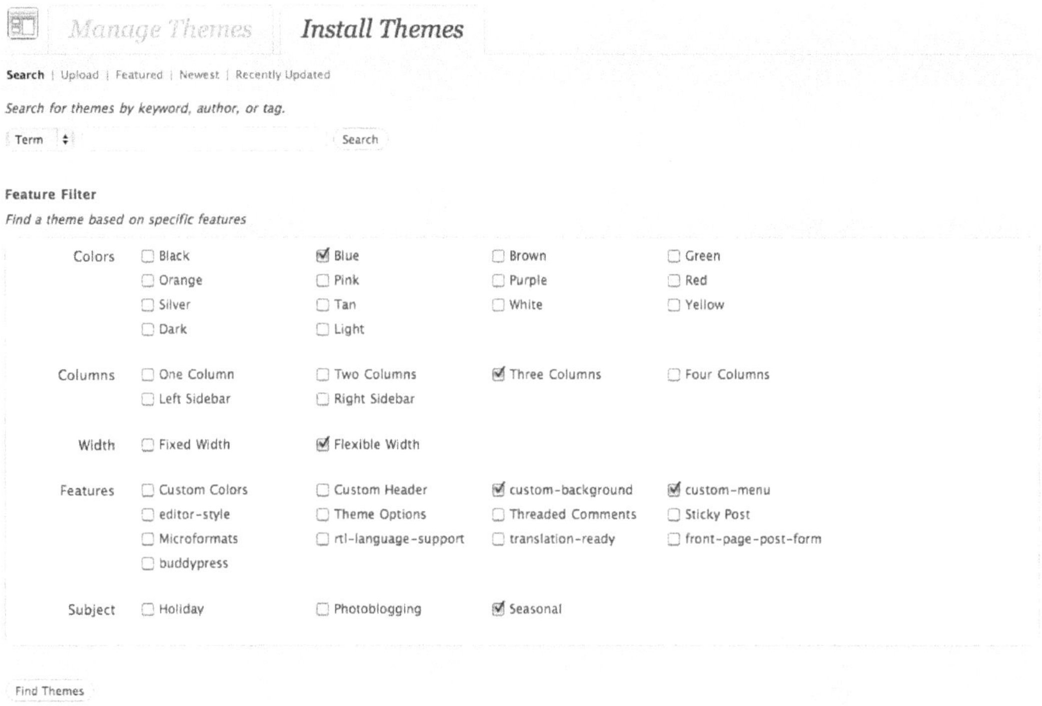

Figure 4.3 Searching themes that have specific features

On selecting the *Find Themes* button, we get a list of themes that satisfy the specified features. The list may appear as shown in Figure 4.5. With every theme, we find three links, *Install, Preview* and *Details* that can be used to install the theme, look at its real-time preview and see more details of the theme, respectively.

Note: We can also download themes to upload them later. For this, visit `http://wordpress.org/extend/themes` for freely available themes.

The *Install Themes* tab also displays six links, namely, Search, Search Results, Upload, Featured, Newest and Recently Updated. A short description of each of these links is as follows:

- **Search**—Displays a page to search for themes by keyword, author or tag. Also displays several checkboxes to specify features such as color, columns, width, features and subject of the theme that we are looking for.

- **Search results**—Displays the themes that satisfy the search criteria.

- **Upload**—Uploads the previously downloaded theme files to our server's `wp-content/themes` folder. We get a dialog box to specify the name of the theme in zip format as shown in Figure 4.4. After specifying a theme file, select the *Install Now* button to upload and install the theme. Once a theme is installed, we can activate it any time to apply it to our blog.

- **Featured**—Displays the featured themes.

- **Newest**—Lists the latest themes added to the WordPress.

- **Recently Updated**—Lists the themes that have been updated recently by their designers.

Figure 4.4 Uploading and installing a theme

On selecting the *Find Themes* button after specifying the features (refer to Figure 4.3), the themes that satisfy the given criteria are listed as shown in Figure 4.5.

Figure 4.5 List of themes that meet the criteria of the specified features

From the list of displayed themes, we can install any one of them by selecting the *Install* link. Let us apply a theme named *Amazing Grace* by *Vladimir Prelovac* on our blog. For more information of the theme, visit the site, http://www.prelovac.com/vladimir. To apply the theme, all we need to do is select the *Install* link of the *Amazing Grace* theme. The theme gets automatically installed on our server and displays three links, *Preview, Activate* and *Return to Theme installer* as shown in Figure 4.6.

Figure 4.6 Links displayed by the installed theme

The *Preview* link gives us a glimpse of our blog when the specified theme will be applied. The *Activate* link applies the selected theme to our blog and the appearance of header, footer, background, layout, etc. of our blog are modified as per the applied theme. Since only one theme can be active at a time, any theme that was active previously gets automatically deactivated. The *Return to Theme Installer* link takes us back to the page that displays the themes that satisfy our search criteria. With the theme *Amazing Grace* applied, our blog may appear as shown in Figure 4.7. We can see that the appearance of our blog is totally changed when we compare it with the blog in the *Twenty Ten* theme shown in Figure 2.12 of Chapter 2.

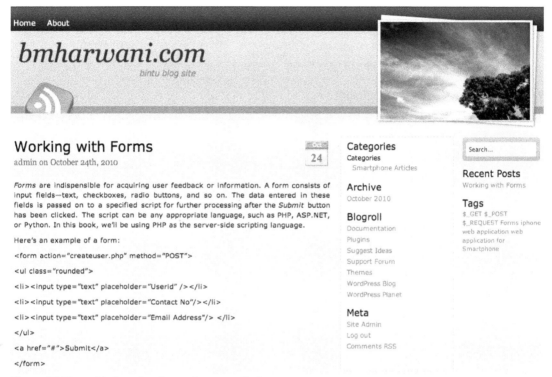

Figure 4.7 Blog with Amazing Grace theme applied

Now, there are two themes installed on our server: *Twenty Ten* and *Amazing Grace* with *Amazing Grace* theme being active at the moment (refer to Figure 4.7). The *Manage Themes* tab displays the two themes as shown in Figure 4.8.

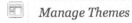 **Manage Themes** Install Themes

Current Theme

 Amazing Grace 3.6 by Vladimir Prelovac

Amazing Grace is a lightweight, super-optimized WordPress theme packed with features (SEO, Adsense, Translation and Widget Ready). Brought to you by Vladimir Prelovac

All of this theme's files are located in /themes/amazing-grace .

Tags: three-columns, fixed-width, threaded-comments, custom-menu, sticky-post, translation-ready, green, brown, yellow, light, tan

Available Themes

Twenty Ten 1.0 by the WordPress team

The 2010 default theme for WordPress.

Activate | Preview | Delete

All of this theme's files are located in /themes/twentyten .

Tags: black, blue, white, two-columns, fixed-width, custom-header, custom-background, threaded-comments, sticky-post, translation-ready, microformats, rtl-language-support, editor-style

There is a new version of Twenty Ten available. View version 1.1 Details or upgrade automatically.

Figure 4.8 Manage Themes tab displaying two themes that are installed on our server

We can again make the previous theme, *Twenty Ten* active by selecting its *Activate* link. We can also delete it from our server by selecting its *Delete* link.

Note: When we activate a theme, any previously active theme gets automatically deactivated.

Though the next menu option in the *Appearance* menu is *Widgets* (Figure 4.1), we will first understand the *Menus* option as it will help us better *understand* the *Custom Menu Widget* option of *Widgets*. The *Menus* option of the *Appearance* menu is used for creating custom menu(s) for our blog. Let us understand how custom menus are created.

4.2 Menus

Menus are used for creating custom menu(s) on our blog. A menu is nothing but a collection of links displayed on our blog. The links can be internal links to the pages, posts or categories of our blog or external links pointing to other sites. To create a custom menu, we select the *Appearance->Menus* option from the *main navigation menu*. On doing this, we get a screen as shown in Figure 4.9.

Depending on the currently active theme, our blog may have one or two custom menus also known as *navigation menus*. For example, the theme *Twenty Ten* supports one menu whereas the theme, *Amazing Grace*, which is currently active on our blog, supports two menus. By default, the two custom or navigation menus are termed as *Top Navigation* and *Bottom Navigation*, respectively. We can always create more custom menus and assign whatever name we like to them.

Figure 4.9 Menus page for creating and managing custom menus

We can make the pages, categories and custom links to appear on the either menu. The right-hand side of the screen shows the contents of the two default custom menus, *Bottom Navigation* and *Top Navigation*. By selecting the + *(plus)* tab on the top right, we can create more custom menus as we will see later. On the left-hand side, we see three sections by default, *Custom Links, Pages* and *Categories*.

The *Pages* and *Categories* section displays the pages and categories that exist on our blog. The *Pages* section displays the two pages provided by default, *Home* and *About*. The *Categories* section displays the *Smartphone Articles* category that we created in Chapter 2. To add a link, i.e., a menu item to any menu, all we need is to activate the desired menu from the right-hand side and select the desired link from under the *Custom Links, Pages* and *Categories* sections that exists on left-hand side followed by selecting *Add to Menu* button. For example, to add a link for the category *Smartphone Articles* to the *Bottom Navigation* menu, we select the *Bottom Navigation* tab from the right-hand side to make it active, select the *Smartphone Articles* checkbox under the *Categories* section followed by selecting *Add to Menu* button.

Brief description of the sections:

- The *Theme Locations* section displays the drop down menus that specify the location of custom menu(s) on the blog.

- The *Custom Link* section is used for linking external URLs to the menu.

- The *Pages* section is for adding links of the published pages in the menu.

- The *Categories* section is for displaying links of the existing categories in the menu.

We can have two more sections, *Posts* and *Post Tags* in the list of existing sections by checking the respective checkboxes in *the Screen Options* (refer to Figure 4.11). The *Posts* and *Post Tags* sections display the posts and post tags of our blog, respectively to be linked to the custom menu.

Note: The Screen Options can be found at the top right corner of the screen

---

The *Top Navigation* menu usually contains links to the two default pages of our blog, *Home* and *About*. To, see the links or menu items that are present on the *Top Navigation* menu, let us select its tab from the right-hand side. We get information of the two links as shown in Figure 4.10.

Figure 4.10 Links in the Top Navigation menu

Note: The *URL* option of the *Home* page displays the URL of the blog.

We can see that the links displayed in Figure 4.10 have some options such as *Navigation Label, Title Attribute*, etc. To configure the links better, we can increase the number of options by checking the checkboxes shown under the *Show advanced menu properties* of the *Screen Options* (Figure 4.11) that is, by checking the checkboxes *Link Target, CSS Classes, Link Relationship (XFN)* and *Description*, we can display four more options besides the two options *Navigation Label* and *Title Attribute*.

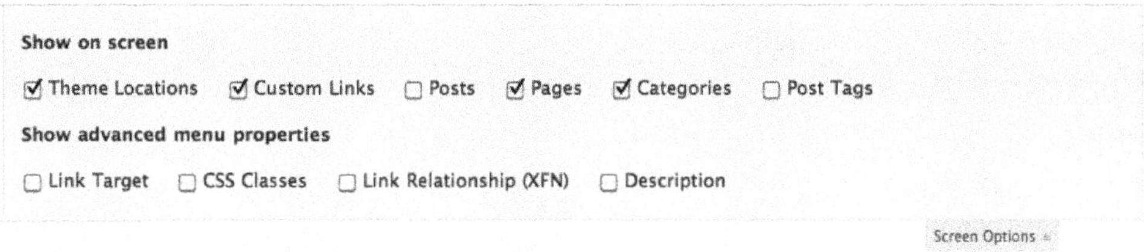

Show on screen

☑ Theme Locations   ☑ Custom Links   ☐ Posts   ☑ Pages   ☑ Categories   ☐ Post Tags

Show advanced menu properties

☐ Link Target   ☐ CSS Classes   ☐ Link Relationship (XFN)   ☐ Description

Screen Options ▲

Figure 4.11 Screen Options page

The usage of different options of the menu item is as follows:

- **Navigation Label**—Enter or edit the text for the menu item.

- **Title Attribute**—Enter the attribute required while displaying the navigation label.

- **Link Target**—Displays two options, *Same window or tab* and *New window or tab* to determine whether we want to display the linked menu item in the same browser window or in the new browser window.

- **CSS Classes (optional)** —Specify the CSS classes to be applied to the linked menu item to enhance its appearance.

- **Link Relationship (XFN)** —Specify the XFN attribute that defines our relation with the author or owner of the linked menu item. Recall that in Figure 3.10, we saw different XFN attributes such as, *Identity, Friendship, Physical, Professional, Geographical, Family* and *Romantic*. We need to enter one of these attributes here.

- **Description**—Enter small description of the menu item. Some themes display the description in the menu.

- **Original**—Displays a link to the original source of the menu item.

- **Remove**—Used to remove the current menu item from the menu.

- **Cancel**—Used to cancel the configuration of the menu item.

Let us keep the *Top Navigation* menu unchanged displaying the links to the two pages, *Home* and *About* and try adding two links to the *Bottom Navigation* menu.

4.2.1 Adding links to menu

Suppose, we wish to add the following two links to the Bottom Navigation menu:

- A Custom link to an external website and
- A link to the category *Smartphone Articles* that we created in Chapter 2.

To add these two links, we follow the following steps:

1. The first step is to select the *Bottom Navigation* tab from the right-hand side (refer to Figure 4.9) to make it active.

2. From the left-hand side, select the *Custom Links* section. In the *URL* field, enter the URL of the website or page to which we want to link. Assuming that I want to link to my website, we will enter its URL, http://bmharwani.com in the *URL* field (refer to Figure 4.12).

Figure 4.12 Options of the Custom Links

3. In the *Label* field, enter the menu item text. Since the custom link points at my website, let us enter the label as *My WebSite*.

4. Finally select the *Add to Menu* button. We find that a link to my website appears on the right-hand side under the *Bottom Navigation* menu labeled *My WebSite* (refer to Figure 4.13).

5. To add a link to the post category in the menu, select the *Categories* section.

6. The only category in our blog, *Smartphone Articles*, gets displayed under the *Categories* section. To add the link for the category in the menu, all we need to do is to select the checkbox to the left of the *Smartphone Articles* category followed by selecting the *Add to Menu* button.

7. Both the custom and category links appear in the *Bottom Navigation* menu found on the right-hand side of the Menus page. We need to save the menu by selecting the *Save Menu* button. A message appears to confirm that the new links are saved in the menu.

After performing these steps, the category link, *Smartphone Articles* and the custom link *My WebSite* appears on the *Bottom Navigation* menu as shown in Figure 4.13.

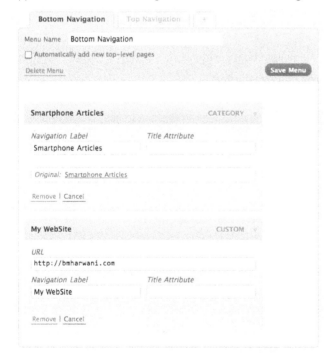

Figure 4.13 Links in the Bottom Navigation menu

Our blog now displays two menus, *Top Navigation* and *Bottom Navigation*. The *Top Navigation* menu displays links to the two pages, *Home* and *About* whereas the *Bottom Navigation* menu displays the link to the post category, *Smartphone Articles* and custom link to *My WebSite* as shown in Figure 4.14.

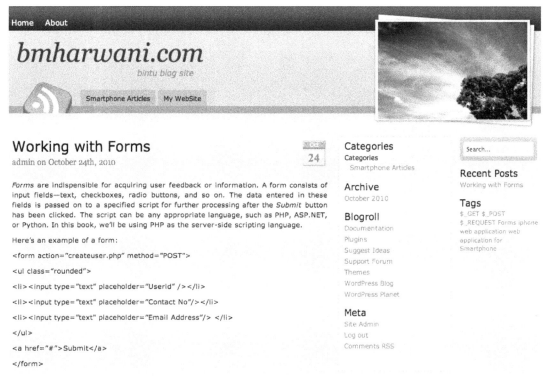

Figure 4.14 Blog displaying the Top and Bottom Navigation menu

In all the sections, whether it is *Custom Links, Pages, Categories, Posts or Post Tags,* we find links such as *Most Used, View All, Search* and *Select All.* Let us understand the meaning of these links with reference to the *Pages* section.

The *Most Recent* and *View All* links display the most recently used pages and all pages of our blog, respectively. The *Search* link displays a box and on entering any text in the box displays all the pages that contain the entered text. The *Select All* link checks the checkboxes of all pages to be added to the active menu.

In this section, we learned to add links to the default custom or navigation menus named *Top navigation* and *Bottom Navigation*. What if we want to have a custom menu by the name we prefer? Let us see how to do that in the following section.

4.2.2. Adding a custom menu

To add a custom menu by any name that we would prefer, we need to select the + *(plus)* tab found besides the Bottom and Top Navigation tabs on the right-hand side of the Menus page (refer to Figure 4.9). On selecting the + *(plus)* tab, we get a screen to specify the name of the custom menu as shown in Figure 4.15.

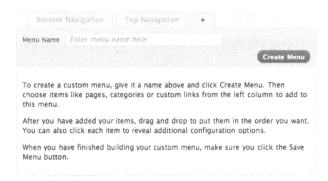

Figure 4.15 Screen for creating a new custom menu

To create a custom menu by the name *Links menu*, we just need to enter the label *Links menu* in the *Menu Name* input field and select the *Create Menu* button. A new tab by the name *Links menu* appears besides the *Bottom Navigation* and *Top Navigation* tabs to inform that the custom menu is created as shown in Figure 4.16.

Figure 4.16 Screen confirming the creation of the custom menu: Links menu

Now, we can add links to the newly created custom menu in the same way we added links to the Bottom navigation menu above. Since, we are happy with the two custom menus, *Top Navigation* and *Bottom Navigation* and do not need the *Links menu* any more, let us delete it by selecting the link *Delete Menu* option shown in Figure 4.16.

WordPress provides a feature known as Widgets for displaying the important content of our blog on the sidebars. The content that the visitor wish to immediately see while opening our blog, such as recent posts, pages, search box, links, etc. are considered important and it is better to display them on the sidebars so that visitor do not have to hunt for them. Let us go ahead and understand Widgets.

4.3 Widgets

A theme has 1 or 2 sidebars where sidebars are the narrow columns to the left or right of our blog posts. The sidebars can be used to display some content such as archives, recent posts, comments, links, calendar, custom menu, etc. The content can be displayed on the sidebars through sections known as widgets. Hence, widgets can be defined as the collection of sections that we can apply to our blog to add and enhance its features.

WordPress provides several built-in widgets. We can also download more from the plug-in repository. Also some themes come with their own widgets. We can configure widgets, add, remove and even move them up or down in the sidebars.

To use widgets in our blog, we select the *Appearance* menu from the *main navigation menu* followed by selecting the *Widgets* option from the submenu options that pops up. We get a list of *available* and *inactive* widgets as shown in Figure 4.17. On the right-hand side is a drop zone for each sidebar, *Left Sidebar* and *Right Sidebar*. The number of sidebars varies on the basis of the theme selected. To display a widget in our blog, we just need to drag it from the list of *Available Widgets* into one of the sidebars. The widgets must be dragged and dropped in the order we want them to appear on the sidebars. Each widget dropped in the sidebar displays a drop down menu to its right which when clicked displays the options screen of the widget. The options screen helps in configuring the widget. To remove a widget from the sidebar, drag it either back to the *Available Widgets* area or into the *Inactive Widgets* area. This way the widget will no longer be displayed.

The settings of the widget that is removed from the sidebars are saved automatically, i.e., its settings will not be lost while dragging it to the *Inactive Widgets* area. When a theme is changed, all the active widgets are moved to the *Inactive Widgets* area. To display the widgets in a new theme, all we have to do is just drag them back into the appropriate sidebars without the need of configuring them again.

Widgets

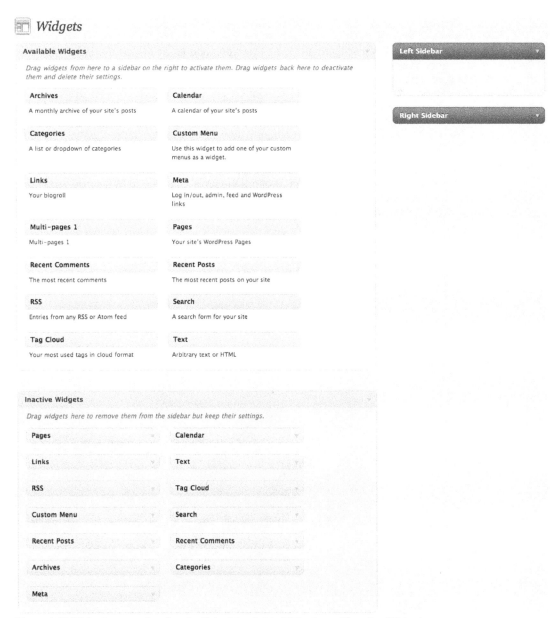

Figure 4.17 Widgets page showing the list of Available Widgets and Inactive Widgets

The list of available widgets and their usage is as follows:

- **Archives**—To display chronological and categorized archives of our publishing history so that the visitors can access it by date and category.

- **Calendar**—Displays a calendar that highlights each day of the week on which we have published a post. Those days are also linked to the post.

- **Categories**—Displays different categories to which posts are assigned. The posts of our blog are organized into categories so that the visitors get all the matter related to a topic at one place.

- **Custom Menu**—Displays the links of the selected custom menu on the sidebars.
- **Links**—Displays all links defined in our blog or of the specified category.
- **Meta**—Displays links to perform meta-functions such as administering the blog, logging in and out, handling RSS, comments, etc.
- **Multi-pages 1—Helps in organizing pages of our blog in the sidebars.**
- **Pages**—Displays links to each page of our blog.
- **Recent Comments**—Displays the list of most recent approved comments of our blog.
- **Recent Posts**—Displays the list of most recent posts published on our blog.
- **RSS**—Displays RSS feed to display content from another blog.
- **Search**—Displays a Search box to search for the desired content on our blog.
- **Tag Cloud**—Displays a tag cloud from all tags. Tag clouds change the size of each tag based on the quantity of its use in our content. Top 45 used tags will be displayed in the tag cloud.
- **Text**—To type short text or HTML code to insert a hyperlink, an image file, etc.

Let us understand these widgets in detail.

4.3.1 Archives Widget

The Archives Widget displays chronological and categorized archives of our publishing history so that the visitors can access it by date and category. The options of archives widget (Figure 4.18(a)) allow us to configure a title, display post counts, their mode of display, i.e., whether to display the archives in drop down or hierarchical manner, etc. The default mode of display is hierarchical. Assuming our post, *Working with Forms* is published in the October month of the year 2010, the archives widget in hierarchical mode appears as shown in Figure 4.18(b). All the month names (along with the year) in which posts were published will be displayed and we can select a month to see all the posts published in that month. In the drop down mode, the archives widget appears as shown in Figure 4.18(c). On selecting the drop down menu, all the month names (along with the year) in which posts were submitted will be displayed for us to select.

Note: We need to select the *Save* button to save the configuration of the widget.

(a)   **(b)**   **(c)**

Figure 4.18 (a) Options of Archives Widget (b) Archives in hierarchical mode (c) Archives in drop down mode

4.3.2 Calendar Widget

The Calendar widget displays a calendar that highlights the days on which the posts were published. The days are also hyperlinked to the respective post(s). The options of the calendar widget (Figure 4.19(a)) allow us to assign a title to the calendar if desired. In the calendar displayed (Figure 4.19(b)), we can see that 24 is highlighted as we published our post *Working with Forms* on that day. On selecting day 24, this post gets displayed.

(a)   (b)

Figure 4.19 (a) Options of Calendar Widget (b) Calendar highlighting the day when post was published

4.3.3 Categories Widget

Recall how we categorized our posts in different categories for the convenience of the visitors. The idea is that the visitors get all the posts related to a subject at one place. The Categories Widget displays all the categories of our blog either in hierarchical or in drop down mode. The options of the categories widget (Figure 4.20(a)) allow us to configure a title, display, the post counts and mode of display. If we do not specify the title, the default title Categories gets assigned to the widget. On checking the checkboxes, *Show post counts* and *Show hierarchy*, the categories of our blog gets displayed in hierarchical mode with the number of posts assigned to it in parenthesis as shown in Figure 4.20(b).

Up till now, we have published a single post, *Working with Forms* assigned to *Smartphone Articles* category. On selecting the checkbox, *Show as dropdown*, the categories appear as a drop down menu as shown in Figure 4.20(c).

(a)   (b)   (c)

Figure 4.20 (a) Options of Categories Widget (b) Categories in hierarchical mode (c) Categories in drop down mode

4.3.4 Custom Menu Widget

The custom menu that we created for our blog can be made visible on the sidebars through this widget. The options displayed by this widget (Figure 4.21(a)) prompts us for the *Title* of the custom menu. The *Select Menu* drop down allows us to decide the links of the menu that we want to display on the sidebars. i.e., we can determine whether to display the links of *Top Navigation* or *Bottom Navigation* menu on the sidebars.

(a)   (b)   (c)

Figure 4.21 (a) Options of Custom Menu Widget (b) Links of Top Navigation menu (c) Links of Bottom Navigation menu

Recall that the *Top Navigation* menu contains links of two pages, *Home* and *About* (refer to Figure 4.9) and the *Bottom Navigation* menu contains a category link, *Smartphone Articles* and a custom link, *My WebSite*. On selecting the *Top Navigation* from the *Select Menu* drop down, the links of the two pages, *Home* and *About* appear on the sidebars as shown in Figure 4.21(b). If we select *Bottom Navigation* from the *Select Menu* drop down, the links defined in it such as the category link, Smartphone Articles and the custom link, My WebSite gets displayed (Figure 4.21(c)).

4.3.5 Links Widget

The Links widget displays the link category with all the links defined in it. WordPress provides a link category by default that is known as the *Blogroll*. The options displayed by this widget include a drop down menu to select the link category (Figure 4.22(a)) that we want to display. It displays three options at the moment, *All Links*, *Blogroll* and *My Articles*. Recall, in Chapter 3, we created a link category named *My Articles*. The *All Links* option displays all links from both link categories, *Blogroll* and *My Articles*. The option *Blogroll* displays all the default links provided by the WordPress in this link category as shown in Figure 4.22(b).

Figure 4.22 (a) Options of Links Widget (b) Links Widget displaying links of Blogroll

Selecting the option *My Articles* from the drop down menu displays the link, *Forward Navigation Via Toolbar Buttons* (refer to Figure 4.23(a)) that we added to this link category in Chapter 3. *The Show Link Image* checkbox displays the image specified by the image address of the link. Recall, we specified the image of the link by specifying its URL in the Image Address box (refer Figure 3.10). The *Show Link Name* checkbox displays the title name assigned to the link. On hovering over the link, its description gets displayed as shown in Figure 4.23(b). The *Show Link Description* checkbox displays a short description of the link along with the link name. The *Show Link Rating* displays the rating assigned to the link as shown in Figure 4.23(c).

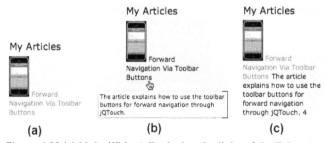

Figure 4.23 (a) Links Widget displaying the links of the link category, My Articles (b) Description of the link is displayed on hovering over it (c) Link name, its description and rating being displayed

4.3.6 Meta Widget

The Meta widget is used for displaying links used for meta-functions such as administering the blog, logging in and out of the blog, accessing RSS feeds and WordPress site from the sidebar. The options of Meta Widget (Figure 4.24(a)) prompt us for the title of the Meta widget. If we do not specify the title, the default title *Meta* appears on the sidebars above the links. We can see, the links shown in Figure 4.24(b) are meant for doing tasks such as administering the blog, logging in and out of the blog, accessing RSS feeds, etc.

| (a) | (b) |

Figure 4.24 (a) Options of Meta Widget (b) Links of Meta Widget displayed in sidebars.

4.3.7 Multi-pages Widget

Multi-pages widget makes it easy for us to organize pages of our blog into the sidebars. We can specify the headpages, the pages to be excluded and the Post IDs. Not only this, we can also display the pages arranged on the basis of Page title, Page order and Page ID where Page order refers to the order in which they appear on the *page management screen*.

To know ID of any page, hover over its title on the page management screen and in the status bar, its link will appear somewhat as follows:

```
Go to "http://example.com/blog/wp-admin/post.php?post=2&action=edit"
```

Where `post=2` specifies that the ID of the page is 2

Similarly, we can find the ID of any post by hovering over it on the posts management screen and viewing at its link in the status bar.

Note that we have an *About* page on our blog. However, it will not be sufficient for trying multi-pages widget. Therefore, let us create four more dummy pages, titled, *Page 1, Page 2, Page 3* and *Page 4*. After creating the four pages, we are ready to try Multi-pages widget. So, drag it from the *Available Widgets* list and drop it on either sidebars. From the Multi-pages Widget's options (Figure 4.25(a)), let us set the *Title* of the widget to appear on the sidebar as *Multi Pages*. In the blog, we will see all the pages from 1 to 4 along with the About page appearing under the heading *Multi Pages* (Figure 4.25(b)). Assuming that the ID of the page titled *Page 3* is 484, if we enter this number in the *Exclude* field, the link of the Page 3 disappears from the widget in the sidebar as shown in Figure 4.25(c).

Multi-pages 1: Multi Pages

Title : Multi Pages
Optional.

Headpage:
Page IDs, separated by commas.

Exclude:
Page IDs, separated by commas.

or

Post IDs:
Posts IDs, separated by commas.

Sort by: Page title

Delete | Close   Save

Multi Pages
About
Page 1
Page 2
Page 3
Page 4

Multi Pages
About
Page 1
Page 2
Page 4

| (a) | (b) | (c) |

Figure 4.25 Links in Top Navigation menu

4.3.8 Pages Widget

The pages widget is used for displaying links to the pages of our blog on the sidebars. The options (Figure 4.26(a)) of this widget prompt us for the title of the widget. If we do not specify the title for this widget, the title displayed by default is *Pages* (refer to Figure 4.26(b)). As in the previous section, the pages being displayed through the widget can be sorted on the basis of Page title, Page order or Page ID where Page order refers to the order in which they appear on the page management screen. We can even exclude the page(s) links from appearing on the sidebars by specifying their IDs in the *Exclude* box. If we wish to exclude more than one page, their IDs need to be separated by comma.

(a)   (b)

Figure 4.26 (a) Options of Pages Widget (b) Output of Pages Widget showing links to the pages

4.3.9 Recent Comments Widget

The Recent Comments Widget helps us display the list of most recent approved comments of our blog on the sidebars. The options displayed by this widget (Figure 4.27(a)) prompts us to specify the title for the comments to be displayed. If we do not specify the title of the widget, the default title displayed is *Recent Comments*. By default, at most five comments are displayed through this widget but we can change the limit of the number of comments being displayed by entering the desired value in the *Number of comments to show* box. Since, we have one approved comment for the post, *Working with Forms*; the widget displays the comment on the sidebars as shown in Figure 4.27(b). We can see that both the commenter and the title of the commented post are displayed. On selecting the post title, the comment(s) gets displayed.

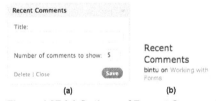

(a)   (b)

Figure 4.27 (a) Options of Recent Comments Widget (b) Recent comments displayed on the sidebar

4.3.10 Recent Posts Widget

The Recent Posts widget allows us to display the most recent posts published on our blog on the sidebars. The titles of the posts gets displayed which can then be selected to view the complete post. Using the options box of this widget (Figure 4.28(a)), we can display a desired title for the Posts displayed on the sidebars by specifying it in the *Title* box. Also, we can limit the number of posts titles being displayed through the *Number of posts to show box*. By default, at most five post titles are allowed to be displayed. Figure 4.28(b) displays the only post of our blog, *Working with Forms* as the recent post.

Recent Posts
Working with Forms

(a)   (b)

Figure 4.28 (a) Options of Recent Posts Widget (b) Links to the recent posts of the blog displayed on the sidebar

4.3.11 RSS Widget

RSS stands for 'Really Simple Syndication'. It is a standardized format for sharing content on the web. The RSS Widget is used to show the contents from other sites into our blog. That is, we can see the fresh contents of the specified site on our blog without even visiting that site. To fetch and import RSS feed from a site, we need a RSS feed URL. Finding RSS feed URL is very easy. For example, to get the RSS feed URLs concerning to sports, just search for "RSS feed URL sports" and we get a list of sites providing the same. In the site, look for the standard feed icon or the word "subscribe" or "feed" and copy the RSS feed URL.

We need to perform the following steps for displaying feeds from other site:

1. In the RSS Widget options (Figure 4.29(a)), paste the RSS feed URL into the first input field. We will be using the following RSS feed URL for sports news:

   `http://rss.cnn.com/rss/edition_sport.rss`

2. Enter the title for the RSS feed. Since our feed is meant for displaying sports news, let us enter the title as *Sports News*.

3. Specify the number of entries from the feed to show in the sidebar. Default number is 5.

4. Check the *Display item content?* checkbox to show a brief description of the post in addition to its title.

5. Check the *Display item author if available?* checkbox to display the author's name.

6. Check the *Display item date?* checkbox to display the date when the post was published.

The output that we might get on checking all the three checkboxes is as shown in Figure 4.29(b). We can see that along with the title, a small description of the post is also displayed. The author of the post is not available, hence is not displayed whereas we can see the date when the post was published. To see the title of the post without its description, we just need to uncheck the checkbox, *Display item content?* The RSS feed that is displayed will now just consist of post title and date when it was published as shown in Figure 4.29 (c).

Figure 4.29 (a) Options of the RSS Widget (b) RSS feeds with item content, author and date (c) RSS feeds with item author and item date.

4.3.12 Search Widget

The Search widget is used for displaying a search box in the sidebar that the visitors can use for searching the desired contents on the blog. The option box of the widget appears as shown in Figure 4.30(a). In the *Title* box, we can enter the title that we want to display above the search box. If we leave the title box empty, the default title that is displayed is *Search for:* as shown in Figure 4.30(b).

Figure 4.30 Options of the Search Widget (b) Search box displayed on the sidebar

4.3.13 Tag Cloud Widget

The Tag Cloud widget displays a tag cloud on the sidebar of our blog. The tag cloud is a collection of tags that we have assigned to our posts. The frequently used tags get displayed in large size. On selecting a tag, all the posts to which the selected tag was assigned gets displayed. The tag cloud not only helps the visitors in finding the posts with the specified keyword but also gives them an idea of the subjects that we frequently post about. At most 45 of our most popular tags get displayed.

The options of the Tag Cloud widget (Figure 4.31(a)) prompts us for the title to be displayed above the tag cloud. If we leave the *Title* box empty, the default title displayed will be either *Tags* or *Categories* depending on the option selected from the *taxonomy* drop down menu. Taxonomy is a technique of classifying things. The posts of our blog can be classified by assigning it to a category or specifying tags for it. The taxonomy drop down menu helps us in determining whether we want to classify the posts of our blog on the basis of categories or tags.

| (a) | (b) | (c) |

Figure 4.31 Options of the Tag Cloud Widget   (b) Tags assigned to the posts displayed on sidebars (c) Categories of the blog displayed on sidebars

The taxonomy drop down menu displays two options, *Post Tags* and *Categories* each meant for displaying specific contents on the sidebars:

- **Post Tags Taxonomy**—Tags as we know are the keywords that describe our post and are independent of each other and does not follow any hierarchical structure. On selecting the *Post Tags* option from the *Taxonomy* drop down menu, the tags assigned to the posts gets displayed with the default title, *Tags* as shown in Figure 4.31(b).

- **Categories Taxonomy**—Selecting this option groups the posts of our blog on the basis of categories. Categories and subcategories of our blog get displayed in a hierarchical manner on the sidebars. Since, the only post category that we have created in our blog is *Smartphone Articles*; it gets displayed on the sidebars under the default heading *Categories* as shown in Figure 4.31(b). On selecting the *Smartphone Articles* category, all the posts assigned to it get displayed.

4.3.14 Text Widget

The Text widget is used for displaying some short text on the sidebars or for writing certain HTML code to insert a hyperlink, displaying an image file, etc. The option of the Text Widget (figure 4.32(a)) prompts us for the title to be displayed above the widget.

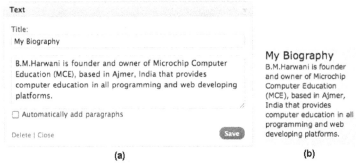

| (a) | (b) |

Figure 4.32 (a) Options of the Text widget (b) Output of the Text widget

The text is added in the large box below the Title box. The checkbox, *Automatically add paragraphs* is checked if we want to display small line space between paragraphs. Figure 4.32 (b) shows the biography displayed on the sidebars.

In order to display an image or hyperlink on the sidebars, we can also write HTML code in the Text widget. Let us assume that I want to display two images with file names *img5a.png* and *manningqeip.png*. Then, before accessing them through HTML code, the two image files must be uploaded on our server through the *Media Library* as discussed in Chapter 3. After uploading the images, we can write HTML codes to display them and can use them to link to some site. A sample HTML code is as given as follows:

```
Beginning Web Development for Smartphones <a
href="http://www.amazon.com/dp/B0042X9CHI"><img src="http://bmharwani.com/blog/wp-
content/uploads/2010/11/img5a.png" </img></a>
```

```
Quick and Easy iPhone Programming <a href="http://manning.com/harwani"><img
src="http://bmharwani.com/blog/wp-content/uploads/2010/11/manningqeip.png" </img></a>
```

The title of the widget is set to *My Latest Books* (refer to figure 4.33(a)). This code displays the book titles along with two images on the sidebars as shown in figure 4.33 (b). The image being hyperlinked navigates us to the target URL when clicked.

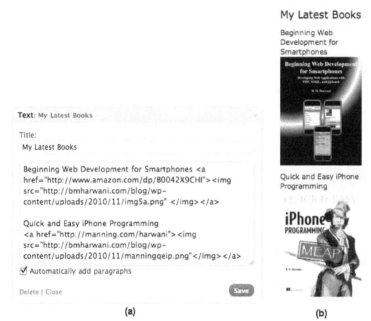

| (a) | (b) |

Figure 4.33 (a) HTML code to display image and hyperlinks through Text Widget (b) Hyperlinked images displayed on the sidebars

After getting hold of the concept of all types of widgets, it is time to apply a few of them to our blog. Let us drag and drop the two widgets, *Archives* and *Categories* on the Left Sidebar and *Recent Posts* widget on the Right Sidebar. The options of the widget as we already know help us in configure the display of widgets. The title of all the three widgets are left blank (refer to Figure 4.34) to display their default titles, which are *Archives*, *Categories* and *Recent Posts,* respectively. The options in the *Archives* widget determine whether we want to display the list of Archives in the form of hierarchy or as a drop down list. Also, the options help us decide whether we want to display the post counts or not.

Let us check the checkbox, *Show post counts* to display the count of the posts in the archives. Also, to display archives in the hierarchical mode (default mode), we leave the checkbox, *Display as a drop down* unchecked. Similarly, to display the categories in the hierarchical mode representing the parent/child hierarchy, along with the count of the posts in each category, we select the two checkboxes, *Show post counts* and *Show hierarchy* from the *Categories Widget's* options. Finally, we want at most 5 recent posts (a default value) to be displayed on the sidebars. So we leave this default value in the *Number of posts to show* field in Recent Posts Widget's options. After setting the options, we save the widget(s) by pressing the *Save* button.

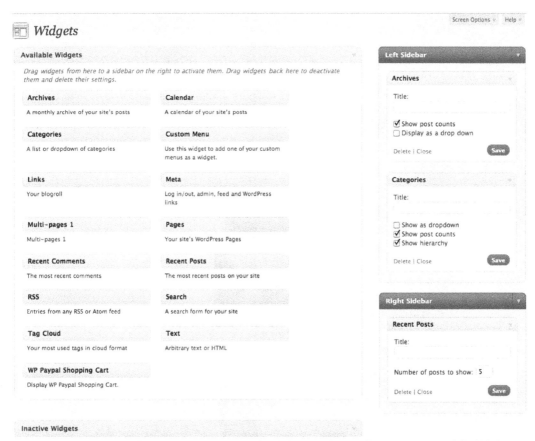

Figure 4.34 Archives and Categories widgets on left sidebar and Recent Posts widget on right sidebar

After applying widgets on the left and right sidebars, our blog appears as shown in Figure 4.35. We see the *Archives* widget displays link, *October 2010 (1)* to inform that a post was published in October month of the year 2010. The *Categories* widget displays the only category in our blog, *Smartphone Articles (1)*. The numerical value (1) in parentheses represents that one post is assigned to the *Smartphone Articles* category. Recall that the post, *Working with Forms* was created and assigned to *Smartphone Articles* category in Chapter 2. The *Recent Posts* widget displays the only post in our blog, *Working with Forms*. Do not be surprised to see the search box in the sidebars as it appears automatically through the current active theme, *Amazing Grace*.

Figure 4.35 Blogs with the three widgets, Archives, Categories and Recent Posts displayed on sidebars

4.4 Using the Theme Editor

WordPress has a built-in theme editor with a syntax highlighting feature. We can view source code of any theme and can edit it using this editor. On selecting the *Appearance->Editor* option from the main navigation menu, *the Edit Themes* page gets opened showing the code of the currently active theme. Figure 4.36 shows the code of the *Amazing Grace* theme. Using the *Select theme to edit:* drop down menu on the top right, we can select any theme that is installed on our server for the purpose of editing.

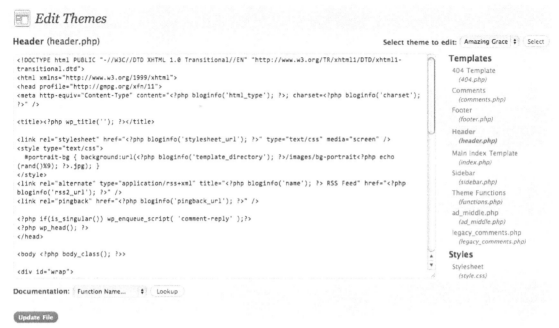

Figure 4.36 Editor displaying the theme code

We must set the permissions of the theme files to make them writable for saving the changes made. The editor lists all files associated with the theme. The *Documentation:* drop down menu displays all the functions that exist in the opened theme file. We can select any function from the *Documentation*: drop down menu followed by selecting the *Lookup* button to see the purpose, description, parameters and return values of the selected function. After editing the code, we save the changes by selecting the *Update File* button.

4.5 Summary

In this chapter we learned how to enhance the appearance of a blog by the application of themes. We also learned to search themes with specific features, and the process of installing, activating and deactivating them. We saw the creation of custom menus and addition and removal of links from them. Next, we learned the usage of each widget in detail. We saw options of each widget and their role in displaying information on sidebars. Finally, we saw how a theme can be edited using a theme editor.

In the next chapter, we will learn to manage users and their profiles. We will also learn to assign different roles to the users depending on their importance

5

Users and Roles

In the previous chapter, we learned the application of themes in making our blog appear dynamic. We also saw the creation of custom menus and its usage in displaying links of categories, pages, etc. in the menus of our blog. We also saw the practical application of each widget in displaying the desired information on sidebars. Finally, we saw how a theme can be edited through a theme editor.

In this chapter we are going to learn:

- **Managing user accounts**—Users are the persons that visit, access, contribute and administer our blog. In this chapter, we will learn how these users are created, edited and deleted.

- **Roles**—The roles are the best mechanism to assign privileges to the users of our blog. In this chapter, we will learn different types of pre-defined roles and the rights or permissions attached to each of them

- **Setting Profiles**—Through Profiles, a user can enter and set personal information; we will see different options that can be set through Profiles.

WordPress provides a very simple mechanism of creating users account, assigning roles and setting profiles. Roles are the easiest and flexible way of controlling access to our WordPress blog as we will see later in this chapter. Recall from Chapter 1, while installation of the WordPress, we were asked for specifying Administrator-username, password and Admin nickname (optional) to access the admin area. At that time, we had specified the Administrator-username as *chirag* (it can be any name) and Admin nickname as *admin* (again it can be any name). Hence, the user *chirag* or *admin* has administrative privileges and can execute any task on the blog such as write and edit posts, create pages, links, categories, link categories, moderate comments, manage plugins, themes, create new user accounts, assign roles to the users, etc.

We can create an unlimited number of user accounts in WordPress with various privileges. Let us see how users are managed in WordPress. On selecting *Users* menu from the main navigation menu, we get the list of options as shown in Figure 5.1.

Figure 5.1 Options in Users menu

5.1 Managing Users

To manage users, i.e., to create new user accounts, changing roles, delete user accounts, etc. we need to open the user's management screen. So, select the *Users->Users* option from the main navigation menu to open the user's management screen. The user's management screen displays the list of existing users in tabular format as shown in Figure 5.2. The table displays the *Username, Name* (first name, last name), *E-mail* address, *Role* and the number of *Posts* published by the user. We can see filter links *All* and

Administrator on the top of the screen that are used to filter the users on the basis of their roles. For example, the filter link, *All* displays all the users of our blog and the *Administrator* link displays the users assigned the Administrator role. At the moment, we see only two filter links in the user's management area, but more links will appear representing other roles such as, *Subscriber, Author, Contributor* and *Editor* when users with these roles are added to the blog.

As filter links represent the roles of the user, they appear as long as there exists at least a single user with a particular role. We can also search for the specific user(s) by entering a string in the Search box followed by selecting the *Search Users* button located at the top right-hand side. All the users containing the entered string in *Username, Name, E-mail*, or *Website* fields get displayed. In case, no match is found, a message *No matching users were found!* is displayed. To delete several users simultaneously, we make use of the *Bulk Actions* drop down menu. For this, all we need to do is to select the checkboxes of the users to which we want to apply the bulk action and select an action from the *Bulk Actions* drop down menu. We can also select all the users displayed in the user's management screen by checking the checkbox in the Table's title, or footer bar. After selecting an action from the *Bulk Actions* drop down menu, we need to select the *Apply* button to execute the action.

The *Change role to* drop down menu besides the *Bulk Actions* is for collectively changing the role of the selected user(s). That is, we select the checkboxes of the users whose roles we want to change and select the desired role from the *Change role to* drop down menu followed by selecting the *Change* button. The *Change role to* drop down displays five pre-defined roles, namely, *Subscriber, Contributor, Author, Editor* and *Administrator*. We will soon see the rights associated with these roles.

Figure 5.2 User's Management Screen

We can see that only one user, the administrator *chirag* is displayed in the user's management area because we have not yet created any new user. Let us now create a new user.

5.2 Creating New Users

To create a new user in WordPress, select the *Users->Add New* option from the main navigation menu. We get the *Add New User* page to enter information of the new user as shown in Figure 5.3.

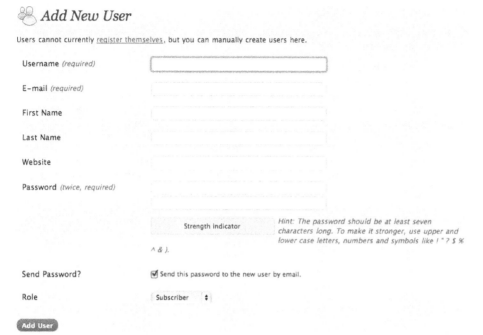

Add New User

Users cannot currently register themselves, but you can manually create users here.

Username *(required)*	
E-mail *(required)*	
First Name	
Last Name	
Website	
Password *(twice, required)*	
	Strength Indicator Hint: The password should be at least seven characters long. To make it stronger, use upper and lower case letters, numbers and symbols like ! " ? $ % ^ &).
Send Password?	☑ Send this password to the new user by email.
Role	Subscriber ⬍

Add User

Figure 5.3 Add New User Page

In the *Add New User* page, we can see that we have to enter a user name, an email address, first name, last name, website URL, password and role of the new user. Out of these fields, the required fields are *Username*, *E-mail*, and *Password*, i.e., these fields cannot be left blank. The checkbox, *Send this password to the new user by email* can be checked if we want an automatic mail be sent to the new user containing his/her password for future reference. The *Role* drop down menu contains five options, *Subscriber*, *Contributor*, *Author*, *Editor* and *Administrator* to be assigned to the new user. The default role of the new user is *Subscriber*. After entering all the information of the new user, select the *Add User* button to create the new user.

Note: Each user's email address must be unique.

The *Add New User* page is used by the administrator for creating user accounts. A visitor can also create his/her account through the blog if we check the *Anyone can register* checkbox in the *General Settings*. These *General Settings* are explained in Chapter 7. After having learned the basics about roles, let us now get into their details.

5.2.1 Roles

Roles are the technique to control the permissions, capabilities or privileges of the users in a blog. Just assigning a role to a user binds him/her to work within the permissions assigned to that role. Hence, we can define a role as a range of tasks that are permitted for any user to perform. The applications of roles relieve the administrator from granting and revoking rights to the individual users for doing specific tasks. WordPress supports five predefined roles:

- **Subscriber**—These users can only manage their own profiles, write or read comments, receive newsletters, etc. but do not have any write permissions.

- **Contributor** —These users can create, edit and delete posts. They can submit posts for editor's approval but cannot publish it.

- **Author**—These users can write, manage and publish posts.

- **Editor**—These users can write and publish posts and pages. They can also publish posts and pages submitted by other users.

- **Administrator**—These users can do all administration tasks and is the main authority of the blog. The *admin* account created during installation is assigned the Administrator role by default. The user with Administrator role can do everything, i.e., can write, edit and approve posts, create pages, links, categories, link categories, moderate comments, manage plugins, themes, users, assign roles to other users, etc.

Now that we have understood the concept of all the fields displayed on the *Add New User* page, let us complete this section by creating a new user by the name *bintu* (or any other you prefer) with its role as *Subscriber*. The user's management screen now displays two users, chirag (administrator) and bintu (Subscriber) as shown in Figure 5.4.

Figure 5.4 User's Management Screen showing two users

Let us now see how to delete a user.

5.3 Deleting Users

There are two ways to delete users from our blog:

- First is by using the *Bulk Actions* drop down button from the user's management screen. To do this, just select the checkboxes of the user(s) that we want to delete and select the delete action from the *Bulk Actions* drop down menu followed by selecting the *Apply* button.

- The second way is to hover the mouse over the user name in the user's management screen and select the Delete link that appears below the user name (refer to Figure 5.4).

On using the above two options, we get a page asking for the action to be taken on the posts and links owned by the user being deleted as shown in Figure 5.5.

Figure 5.5 Delete Users Page asking for the further actions

The page displays the ID of the user and displays two options:

- **Delete all posts and links**—Selecting this option deletes the selected user(s) as well as the posts and links owned by them.

- **Attribute all posts and links to existing user**—Selecting this option attributes all the posts and links of the deleted user(s) to the user selected from the drop down menu.

On selecting either option, we need to select the *Confirm Deletion* button to execute the delete operation. On successful deletion of the user, we get a confirmation message.

5.4 Setting Profiles

Profile is a page where we can enter our personal information and set personal options. Among personal information, we can define our name that appears publicly on our blog, instant messenger IDs, biographical information, etc. In the personal options, we can enable/disable visual editor, choose color scheme for Dashboard, enable/disable keyboard shortcuts, etc. To open the Profile Page, select the *Users->Your Profile* option from the main navigation menu. The Profile Page displays the fields as shown in Figure 5.6.

Note: The personal information asked in Profile page is optional.

Figure 5.6 Profile Page

Personal Options: Here we set the personal options such as enable or disable visual editor, enable or disable keyboard shortcuts, selecting color scheme of our blog, etc. A short description of these options is as follows:

- **Visual Editor**—To use the Visual Editor while writing posts, leave the checkbox, *Disable the visual editor when writing* unchecked.

- **Admin Color Scheme**—It displays options to set the colors in our Dashboard. The default is the Gray color scheme.

- **Keyboard Shortcuts**—Check the checkbox, *Enable keyboard shortcuts for comment moderation* to use keyboard shortcuts while moderating comments. On selecting the *More information* link, we will be navigated to the `codex.wordpress.org/Keyboard_Shortcuts` page that shows the full list of comment moderation shortcuts.

Name: Here, we enter personal information of the user such as first name, last name, nickname and select one out of them to be displayed publicly.

Contact Info: Here, we provide our contact information such as e-mail address, website, and ID for instant messages like Yahoo! IM, AIM (AOL Instant Messenger) and Jabber/Google Talk. The email address is the required field here and the rest of the fields are optional. The email address is required for informing us of new comments posted, new registrations, links set to our posts, etc.

About Yourself: Here, we enter our small biography and can enter a new password if we want to change it. A short description of these options is as follows:

- **Biographical Info**—The biographical information that we will enter here will be picked up by the search engines and will also be shown publicly.

- **New Password**—Enter the new password of the blog if we want to change it. To confirm the new password, we will type it again in the second text box. Below the two password boxes is the *Strength Indicator* that informs if the password entered is secure enough. It is better to use a combination of letters, numbers and symbols to make a strong password.

5.4.1 Editing User

To edit a user, hover the mouse over the user name in the user's management screen (refer to Figure 5.4) and select the *Edit* link that appears below the user name. The profile page of the user gets opened in the edit mode. We can make the desired changes and save the changes by selecting the *Update* button.

5.5 Summary

In this chapter, we learned to create, edit and delete user accounts. We also saw the usage of roles in assigning privileges to the users. Finally, we saw the usage of Profile in keeping personal information of the users.

The next chapter is focused on plugins. That is, we will learn the role of plugins in extending features of our blog. We will also learn to install and activate plugins and see how to delete, upgrade and edit plugins.

6

Using Plugins

In the previous chapter we learned to manage users and saw how to assign roles to them to control their privileges. We also learned to enter personal information on the Profile page.

In this chapter, we are going to extend features of our blog through plugins. We will learn to install and activate plugins. Also, we will see how to delete, upgrade and edit plugins.

Let us first begin with an introduction of plugins.

6.1 Plugins

To add more features to our blog, we take the help of plugins. For example, adding the Shopping Cart feature, or adding the Contact Us form that includes CAPTCHA support, or playing an audio file, are some of the many features that can be added to our blog through plugins. Plugins are codes that interact with WordPress API for the purpose of extending its functionality. That is, through Plugins, we can customize WordPress to suit our needs without altering the core WordPress code. On selecting the Plugins menu from the main navigation menu, we get the options as shown in Figure 6.1.

Figure 6.1 Links in the Plugins menu

6.2 Managing Plugins

To manage plugins, we need to select the first option, *Plugins* from the Plugins menu. We get a *plugins management page* as shown in Figure 6.2, which we will be using extensively for managing plugins. The plugins management page displays the lists of all plugins that are currently installed on our server. All the installed plugins are stored in the *wp-content/plugin* directory of our web server. WordPress installs two plugins on our server by default, namely, *Akismet* and *Hello Dolly*. Both the plugins are in inactive state initially.

- **Akismet** is a plugin that protects our blog from spam. It checks the content of the comment anonymously with an online server to know if it is spam or not.

- **Hello Dolly** plugin randomly displays lyrics from the song sung by Louis Armstrong in the upper right of the admin panel on every page. The reason why this plugin is supplied by default is that the creator of WordPress, Matt Mullenweg, is a big jazz fan.

If the Akismet asks for an API key it means it is not yet setup to block spams. The Akismet needs to be setup to acts as an antispam tool. Let us learn how to set up Akismet.

Note: An extra menu option, Akismet Configuration automatically appears in the Plugins menu if the Akismet is not setup on our blog

Setting Up Akismet

To setup Akismet, go to the site WordPress.com and log in to your account. If the account is not yet created, you will need to sign up to create one. In the main navigation menu hover over the *My Account* link in the top left corner of the window, and select the *Edit Profile* option. A page titled *My Public Profile* gets opened that asks for our basic details. Search and select the link, *API Key and other Personal Settings*. This link can be seen just above the *Update Profile* button. On selecting the link, a page titled *Personal Settings* opens up displaying the API key we are looking for. Copy the API key and return to our blog. In our blog, select the *Plugins -> Akismet Configuration* option from the main navigation menu, enter Akismet API key into the textbox followed by selecting the *Update API Key* button. On doing this, we get a message; *Your key has been verified. Happy blogging!* that means the Akismet is configured and is now active to stop spamming in our blog.

Note: The plugins that are listed with a grey background are inactive plugins and those with a white background are plugins that are active currently.

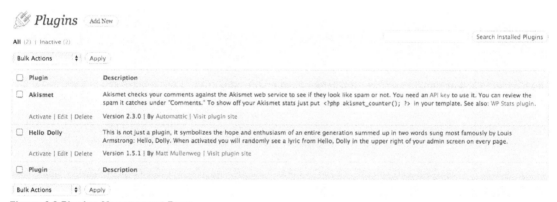

Figure 6.2 Plugins Management Page

The *plugins management page* displays the information of the installed plugins that includes the plugin name, description, author information, and the plugin site. We can filter the plugins by using the filter links, *All, Inactive* and *Upgrade Available* across the top of the page. These links are self-explanatory, the *All* link displays all plugins available on our server, the *Inactive* link displays the plugins that are in inactive state and *Upgrade Available* link displays the plugins whose upgrade is available. We can also search plugins using the search box at the top right of the page. To manage plugins in bulk, select the checkbox to the left of each plugin name, and then select an action (*Activate, Deactivate, Upgrade* or *Delete*) from the *Bulk Actions* drop down menu followed by selecting the *Apply* button. To quickly select all the plugins with a single click, select the checkbox to the left of the *Plugin* column heading.

Beneath every plugin name that is listed in the *plugins management page*, we see the followings links:

- **Activate:** This link appears only below the name of the plugins that are not active. Click the link to activate the plugin.

- **Deactivate:** This link appears only below the name of the plugins that are active. Click the link to deactivate the plugin.

- **Edit:** This link appears below all listed plugins, whether they are active or not. Click the link to visit the *Edit Plugins page*. The *Edit Plugins page* is for editing the individual plugin files.

- **Delete:** This link appears only below the name of the inactive plugins. Click the link to delete the plugin from the blog.

Below the plugin description are the *version number* of the plugin, the plugin *author's name* and a link to the website where we can read more information about the plugin.

6.3 Deleting Plugins

Before deleting a plugin, it has to be deactivated. That is, if any plugin is active, we need to deactivate it first before deleting it. To deactivate an active plugin, hover over its name on the *plugins management page* and select the *Deactivate* link that appears below the name. On selecting the *Deactivate* link, the plugin becomes inactive. To delete an inactive plugin, all we need is to hover over the plugin name and select the *Delete* link from the links that appears below the name. Since, the plugin *Hello Dolly* that is automatically installed on our server is already *inactive*, let us delete it by hovering over its name and selecting the *Delete* link. We get a dialog box asking for confirmation as shown in Figure 6.3.

Figure 6.3 Dialog box asking for confirmation before deleting the plugin

We find two buttons, *Yes, Delete these files* and *No, Return me to the plugin list* where the *Yes, Delete these files* button permanently deletes the plugin from our server and the button, *No, Return me to the plugin list* cancels the delete command and takes us back to the *plugins management page*. Lets delete the Hello Dolly plugin by selecting the *Yes, Delete these files* button.

6.4 Adding Plugins

We can add new plugins either by selecting the *Plugins* menu from the main navigation menu followed by selecting the *Add New* option from the list of options that pop up or by selecting the *Add New* button from the *plugins management page*. Choosing either option opens the *Install Plugins* page as shown in Figure 6.4. *The Install Plugins page* is where we can search for plugins from the WordPress Plugin Directory by keyword, author or tag.

 *Install Plugins*

Search | Upload | Featured | Popular | Newest | Recently Updated

Plugins extend and expand the functionality of WordPress. You may automatically install plugins from the WordPress Plugin Directory or upload a plugin in .zip format via this page.

Search

Search for plugins by keyword, author, or tag.

| Term ♦ | | Search Plugins |

Popular tags

You may also browse based on the most popular tags in the Plugin Directory:

admin AJAX buddypress comment comments content email Facebook feed flash gallery google image images javascript jquery link links media page pages photo photos plugin Post posts rss seo shortcode sidebar social spam statistics stats tags twitter video widget widgets wordpress

Figure 6.4 Install Plugins page

The *Term* drop down menu helps in searching plugins with the desired *keyword, author* or *tag*. For example, to search a plugin with the desired keyword, select the *keyword* option from the *Term* drop down menu and enter the keyword or feature that we want in our plugin and select the *Search Plugins* button. On doing this, we get a list of plugins that has the specified keyword. Similarly, to search for a plugin developed by a specific *author*, select the *Author* option from the *Term* drop down menu and enter the name of the author in the textbox whose plugins we are looking for followed by selecting the *Search Plugins* button. We can also search plugins by tag by clicking on any of the tag names that appear under the *Popular Tags* heading at the bottom of the *Install Plugins* page.

Let us learn the procedure of installing and activating plugins by adding a contact form to our blog. For this, we will need to install a plugin to display the contact form with specific features.

6.4.1 Adding Contact Form to our Blog

Contact Forms are the common means of getting feedback, suggestions and other information from the visitors of our blog. We want that when a user selects the *Contact Us* link in our blog, a contact form must be displayed on the screen that prompts the user for name, email address, subject, suggestion/message/question, etc. Also, to avoid spamming, we would require CAPTCHA support in the contact form. Besides this, we also wish that when a contact form is submitted, the administrator must be informed about it via mail. We would need to search for a plugin that displays a contact form with all the specified features.

To search for the plugins that displays a contact form, we enter the keyword *contact form* in the *Install Plugins* page followed by selecting the *Search Plugins* button. We get a list of plugins that when installed and activated displays a contact form. With every listed plugin name, we find two links, *Details* and *Install Now*. The *Details* link opens a *Description window* displaying information about the selected plugin, version number, author name and an *Install Now* button to install the plugin whereas the *Install Now* link directly installs the plugin on our server.

As an example, I have chosen the plugin, *Fast Secure Contact Form* for displaying contact form in this book as it has all the specified features just discussed and more and is also very easy to implement. On selecting the *Install Now* link of the *Fast Secure Contact Form* plugin, it gets installed on the server. On successful installation of the plugin, we get the Installing Plugins page displaying a confirmation message that the plugin has been downloaded, unpacked and successfully installed. Below this message, the page also displays two links, *Activate Plugin* and *Return to Plugin Installer* as shown in Figure 6.5. The *Activate Plugin* link activates the plugin whereas the *Return to Plugin Installer* link takes us back to the *Install Plugins* page to search and install more plugins.

Installing Plugin: Fast Secure Contact Form 2.9.4.1

Downloading install package from http://downloads.wordpress.org/plugin/si-contact-form.zip...

Unpacking the package...

Installing the plugin...

Successfully installed the plugin Fast Secure Contact Form 2.9.4.1.

Actions: Activate Plugin | Return to Plugin Installer

Figure 6.5 Page showing successful installation of Fast Secure Contact Form plugin

Let us select the *Activate Plugin* link to activate it. On doing this, we will be taken to the *plugins management page* showing all the plugins that are installed on our server as shown in Figure 6.6.

Bulk Actions ⬦ Apply	
☐ **Plugin**	**Description**
☐ **Akismet**	Akismet checks your comments against the Akismet web service to see if they look like spam or not. You need an API key to use it. You can review the spam it catches under "Comments." To show off your Akismet stats just put <?php akismet_counter(); ?> in your template. See also: WP Stats plugin.
Deactivate	Edit	Version 2.4.0	By Automattic	Visit plugin site
☐ **Fast Secure Contact Form**	Fast Secure Contact Form for WordPress. The contact form lets your visitors send you a quick E-mail message. Blocks all common spammer tactics. Spam is no longer a problem. Includes a CAPTCHA and Akismet support. Does not require JavaScript. Settings	Donate
Settings	Deactivate	Edit	Version 2.9.4.1	By Mike Challis	Visit plugin site

Figure 6.6 Plugins Management Page showing newly installed plugin

As expected, we see our plugin, *Fast Secure Contact Form* besides the existing plugin, *Akismet*. The link *Deactivate* below the plugin *Fast Secure Contact Form* confirms that it is currently in active state and will be deactivated on selecting the *Deactivate* link. The *Settings* link displays a *Settings Page* that guides us in configuring the plugin. The *Settings Page* also displays the code that we need to add into a *Page* to convert it into a Contact Form. Through the Settings Page, we can configure following things :

- Enter and edit the welcome message that the visitor gets on opening the Contact Form. The default welcome message displayed by the plugin is, *Comments or questions are welcome* that we can edit if desired.

- Enter and edit the email address of the administrator where visitor's comments will be mailed.

- Hide or show the detailed information of the sender such as his/her IP Address, date, time, etc.

- Turn On or Off Akismet Spam Prevention.

- Enable or disable CAPTCHA.

After configuring the plugin through the Settings Page, the next step is to add a new page to the blog and convert it into a Contact Form by adding the code specified in the Settings Page. So, let us add a new page and set its title to *Contact Us* as shown in Figure 6.7.

Figure 6.7 Writing code to convert a page into the Contact Form page

In the body of the page, we write the code as specified in the Settings Page to convert it into the Contact Us page:

```
[si-contact-form form='1']
```

By adding the above code, the new page gets converted into the Contact Us page. Let us publish the page by selecting the *Publish* button. We find that a new link, *Contact Us* appears in the Bottom Navigation area in our blog besides the two links, *Smartphone Articles* and *My WebSite* as shown in Figure 6.8.

Note: if in case, we do not find the Contact Us link in the Bottom Navigation area, we can manually add it through the *Adding links to menu* section discussed in Chapter 4. Recall that some of the plugins do not appear on the blog automatically but appear on the Widgets page from where they need to be dragged to the sidebars to display and configure.

On selecting the *Contact Us* link from our blog, a contact form opens up displaying a default welcome message, *Comments or questions are welcome* or the one that we specified while configuring the plugin. The contact form displays input fields allowing visitors to enter name, email address, subject, message and CAPTCHA code. The message entered in the contact form is mailed to the administrator when a visitor selects the *Submit* button.

Figure 6.8 Contact Form prompting the user to write and submit a message

A thank you message informing the receipt of the message is displayed to the visitor,

This is how a plugin is installed and activated. Lets install one more that is used to convert categories to tags and vice versa. Recall from Chapter 2, the categories are used for organizing the posts and tags are used for describing the posts. Let us go ahead and install the plugin required to perform this conversion.

6.4.2 Converting categories to tags

The first step for converting categories to tags is to open the *Categories* page to see the categories that exists in our blog. Let us select the *Posts->Categories* option from the main navigation menu to open the *Categories* page. In the *Categories* page (refer to Figure 2.2), on the left-hand side is the area for adding new categories and the right-hand side is the *categories management area*. The categories management area displays the categories in our blog. As expected, we see two categories, *General* and *Smartphone Articles* listed in categories management area. In this area, we can find a link *category to tag converter* that we have to select to begin the process of converting categories to tags. On selecting this link, the *Import* page gets opened showing links to install different importers as shown in Figure 6.9. As our purpose is to convert categories to tags and vice versa, we will need to select the third link, *Categories and Tags* Converter from the *Import* page

Recall, we renamed the default category, *Uncategorized* to *General* in Chapter 2.

Figure 6.9 Import page displaying links to install different importers

We get a dialog box showing description of the importer (plugin), its version, author, compatibility, etc. The dialog box also displays the *Install Now* button that we select to install the plugin to our server. The plugin gets downloaded, unpacked and installed on our server. We get a confirmation message of successful installation of the plugin prompting us to activate it as shown in Figure 6.10.

Figure 6.10 Message displayed on successful installation of plugin

Now, we have two links to select, *Activate Plugin & Run Importer* and *Return to Importers* where the former link activates and executes the plugin to search and display the existing categories to convert them to tags and the latter takes us back to the *Import* page to install more importers. On selecting the *Activate Plugin & Run Importer* link, we get a page displaying all the categories of our blog that may be converted to tags as shown in Figure 6.11.

Categories to Tags   Tags to Categories

🔧 Convert Categories (2) to Tags.

Hey there. Here you can selectively convert existing categories to tags. To get started, check the categories you wish to be converted, then click the Convert button.

Keep in mind that if you convert a category with child categories, the children become top-level orphans.

Check All

☐ General (0)
☐ Smartphone Articles (1)

Convert Categories to Tags

Figure 6.11 Page to convert categories to tags

We can see two categories, *Smartphone Articles* and *General* category where *General* category is the modified name of the default category *Uncategorized* provided by the WordPress. Since, there is no post assigned to *General* category, there is no point converting it into a tag, so we will be converting only the *Smartphone Articles* category to tag. To convert this category let us select its checkbox and then click on the *Convert Categories to Tags* button. On doing this, we get a message of successful conversion of the *Smartphone Articles* category to tag as shown in Figure 6.12.

Categories to Tags   Tags to Categories

Converting category **Smartphone Articles** ... Converted successfully.

We're all done here, but you can always convert more.

Figure 6.12 Page to convert categories to tags

When the category is converted to tag, it gets disappeared from our blog and all the posts assigned to that category are assigned to the *Uncategorized* category. That is, the *Smartphone Article* category disappears from the *Categories* page and in the *post management screen*, the post, *Working with Forms* that was previously assigned to *Smartphone Articles* category is now assigned to the *Uncategorized* category as shown in Figure 6.13.

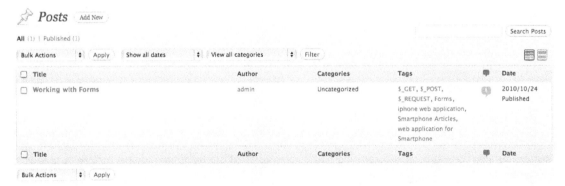

Figure 6.13 Post assigned to the Uncategorized category and its category added to the Tags column

The main thing to observe is that in the *Tags* column, in the list of tags that we defined while publishing the post, one new tag is added, *Smartphone Articles* hence confirming that this category is converted to tag.

Note: When we convert a category with child categories into tag, the children become top-level orphans.

Let us now try the reverse procedure, i.e., convert tags to categories.

6.4.3 Converting Tags to Categories

To convert a tag to category, we need to select the *Tools->Import* option from the main navigation menu. The *Import* page opens up (refer to Figure 6.9). Again, we select the third link, *Categories and Tags Converter* as done earlier. However, since the *Categories to Tag Converter* plugin is already installed on our server, we will not be asked to install the plugin again and a page gets displayed with two buttons at the top, *Categories to Tags* and *Tags to Categories*. On selecting the *Tags to Categories* button, all the tags of all the posts gets displayed. All the tags have a number in parentheses representing the number of posts attached to that tag. We can convert any tag to category by checking its checkbox followed by selecting the *Convert Tags to Categories* button found at the bottom of the page. We get several tags that we had defined for the post, *Working with Forms* along with the newly added tag, *Smartphone Articles* as shown in Figure 6.14.

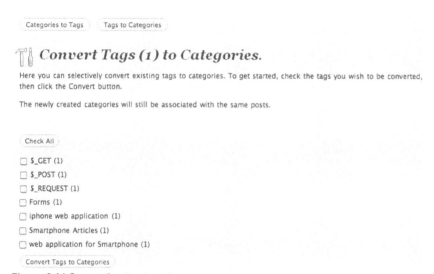

Figure 6.14 Converting tag to category

Let us select the checkbox of the tag *Smartphone Articles* followed by selecting the *Convert Tags to Categories* button. We find that the tag, Smartphone Articles is converted back to category.

6.5 Upgrading a Plugin

WordPress comes with a built-in plugin upgrade feature. When an upgrade of a plugin is available, we are automatically informed about it. A message appears after the Plugins menu showing a circled number representing the number of plugins whose upgrade is available as shown in Figure 6.15.

Figure 6.15 A circled number representing the number of plugins awaiting upgradation

On selecting the circled number, we get a page that displays the links to view the new version details and to upgrade automatically as shown in Figure 6.16.

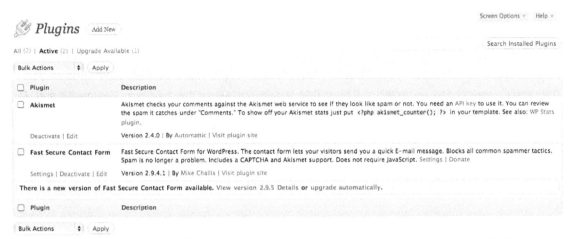

Figure 6.16 Messages displayed on the plugins management screen informing about the new versions that are available of the installed plugins

Figure 6.16 declares that a new version of the plugin, *Fast Secure Contact Form* is available and we can view the details of this new version and can also upgrade to it automatically.

6.6 Using the Plugin Editor

WordPress has a built-in plugin editor with a syntax highlighting feature. We can view source code of any plugin and can edit it using this editor. On selecting the *Plugins->Editor* option from the main navigation menu, the *Edit Plugins* page gets opened showing the code of the first plugin that exists in the plugins management area. Figure 6.17 shows the code of the *Akismet* plugin. Using the *Select plugin to edit:* drop down menu on the top right, we can select the plugin that we want to edit.

 *Edit Plugins*

Editing **akismet/akismet.php** (inactive)   Select plugin to edit: [Akismet ⬍] [Select]

Plugin Files

akismet/akismet.php
akismet/readme.txt

```php
<?php
/*
Plugin Name: Akismet
Plugin URI: http://akismet.com/
Description: Akismet checks your comments against the Akismet web service to see if they look like spam or
not. You need an <a href="http://akismet.com/get/">API key</a> to use it. You can review the spam it catches
under "Comments." To show off your Akismet stats just put <code>&lt;?php akismet_counter(); ?&gt;</code> in
your template. See also: <a href="http://wordpress.org/extend/plugins/stats/">WP Stats plugin</a>.
Version: 2.3.0
Author: Automattic
Author URI: http://automattic.com/wordpress-plugins/
*/

define('AKISMET_VERSION', '2.3.0');

// If you hardcode a WP.com API key here, all key config screens will be hidden
if ( defined('WPCOM_API_KEY') )
        $wpcom_api_key = constant('WPCOM_API_KEY');
else
        $wpcom_api_key = '';

function akismet_init() {
        global $wpcom_api_key, $akismet_api_host, $akismet_api_port;

        if ( $wpcom_api_key )
```

Documentation: [Function Name... ⬍] [Lookup]

[Update File]

Figure 6.17 Editor displaying the plugin code

We must set the permissions of the plugin files to make them writable for saving the changes made. The editor lists all the files associated with a plugin. The *Documentation:* drop down menu displays all the functions that exist in the opened plugin file. We can select any function from the *Documentation:* drop down menu followed by selecting the *Lookup* button to see the purpose, description, parameters and return values of the selected function.

6.7 Summary

In this chapter we learned to handle plugins and their role in extending features of our blog. We also saw how to activate, edit, deactivate and delete plugins.

In the following chapter, we will be learning about tools and settings. We will learn to grab web pages or posts on another site and publish them on our blog. Also, we will learn to import contents from other blogging platforms such as Blogger, LiveJournal, Movable Type and TypePad, RSS and WordPress into our WordPress blog. We will also learn to export our blog contents. Finally, we will learn to configure our WordPress blog through different settings such as General, Reading, Writing, Discussion, Media, Privacy and Permalinks.

7

Tools and Settings

In the previous chapter, we dealt with plugins. We learned to extend features of our blog by installing and activating plugins. We also saw how to deactivate and delete plugins.

In this chapter, we will be covering two important menus, Tools and Settings. Using these menus, we will be learning to:

- Use *Press This* tool to grab web pages found on the net
- Import contents from different blogging platforms into our WordPress blog
- Export contents of our WordPress blog
- Allow visitors to register on our blog
- Set Date and Time format
- Submit posts via email
- Perform remote publishing, i.e., submit posts from a desktop client
- Define default sizes for media files
- Control visibility of our blog
- Generate search engine friendly URLs through Permalink Settings

Let us begin this chapter with the Tools menu.

7.1 Tools

The Tools menu provides the following tools to manage contents of our website:

- **Bookmarklet** that helps us in grabbing pages found on the net and post them to our blog,
- **Multiple plugins** for importing content from different blogging sites such as Blogger, Moveable Type, TypePad, LiveJournal and WordPress into our WordPress blog and
- **Export** feature to export our blog content to an XML file so that it can be used for importing in other blog site.

On selecting the Tools menu, we get the options as shown in Figure 7.1.

Figure 7.1 Options in the Tools menu

On selecting the Tools option, we get a page that shows two tools, *Press This* and *Categories and Tags Converter* as shown in Figure 7.2.

 Tools

Press This

Press This is a bookmarklet: a little app that runs in your browser and lets you grab bits of the web.

Use Press This to clip text, images and videos from any web page. Then edit and add more straight from Press This before you save or publish it in a post on your site.

Drag-and-drop the following link to your bookmarks bar or right click it and add it to your favorites for a posting shortcut.

Press This

Categories and Tags Converter

Use this to convert categories to tags or tags to categories.

Figure 7.2 Tools page

Press This is a bookmarklet built into WordPress that allows us to grab any web page(s) that we find on the net and publish it on our blog. To use this tool, we need to drag the *Press This* link from the *Tools* page and drop it into the bookmarks bar. Other existing bookmarks in the bookmarks bar will automatically shift to accommodate the new link. As soon as we drop it in place, we are prompted to supply its name. By default, it inherits the text of the link as shown in Figure 7.3.

Figure 7.3 Specifying a name to the *Press This* link

Here, we keep the name of the bookmark as *Press This* and select the *OK* button. The *Press This* link appears as bookmark in our bookmarks bar. Now, while surfing the Internet if we find any page or post that we want to publish on our blog, all we need is to select the *Press This* bookmark from the browser's bookmarks bar. It may happen that we get a *404 error*. The error is because of the reason that the URI encoding gets mixed up with the mod_rewrite function. To fix this problem, right-click on the *Press This* bookmark on the browser and select the *Properties* option. Safari users can select the *Edit Address* option. We will find a JavaScript code in the *Location box* (*Address box* in Safari) as shown below:

```
javascript:var%20d=document,w=window,e=w.getSelection,k=d.getSelection,x=d.selection,s=(e
?e():(k)?k():(x?x.createRange().text:0)),f='http://bmharwani.com/blog/wp-admin/press-
this.php',l=d.location,e=encodeURIComponent,u=f+'?u='+e(l.href)+'&t='+e(d.title)+'&s='+e(
s)+'&v=4';a=function(){if(!w.open(u,'t','toolbar=0,resizable=1,scrollbars=1,status=1,widt
h=720,height=570'))l.href=u;};if%20(/Firefox/.test(navigator.userAgent))%20setTimeout(a,%
200);%20else%20a();void(0)
```

In this code search for:

```
u='+e(l.href)+'
```

and replace it with:

```
u='+e(l.href.replace(/\//g,'\\/'))+'
```

The modified JavaScript code appears as:

```
javascript:var%20d=document,w=window,e=w.getSelection,k=d.getSelection,x=d.selection,s=(e
?e():(k)?k():(x?x.createRange().text:0)),f='http://bmharwani.com/blog/wp-admin/press-
this.php',l=d.location,e=encodeURIComponent,u=f+'?u='+e(l.href.replace(/\//g,'\\/'))+'&t=
'+e(d.title)+'&s='+e(s)+'&v=4';a=function(){if(!w.open(u,'t','toolbar=0,resizable=1,scrol
lbars=1,status=1,width=720,height=570'))l.href=u;};if%20(/Firefox/.test(navigator.userAge
nt))%20setTimeout(a,%200);%20else%20a();void(0)
```

After making the above-mentioned changes, select *Save* to save the changes. Our *Press This* bookmark is functional now and while surfing on the net, if we come across a web page that we want to publish on our blog we can just select the *Press This* bookmark from the browser bar. On doing this, a new window gets opened in the WordPress text editor with the imported text as shown in Figure 7.4. We can add more text, edit it, select the category, add our own tags, images or videos, etc.

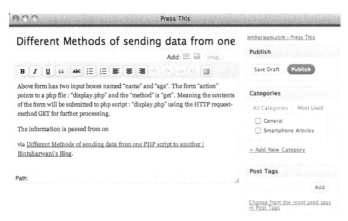

Figure 7.4 Web Page captured through *Press This*

After making the desired changes, we can select the *Save Draft* or *Publish* button to either save the content for future changes or to publish it on our blog straight away. On selecting the *Publish* button, the post gets published on our blog and is confirmed with the message, *Your post has been saved*. The links to view and edit the post are also displayed along with the message. The grabbed page can be seen in our blog as shown in Figure 7.5.

Figure 7.5 Captured Web Page appears on our blog

Hence, we can see that Press This is an excellent tool for publishing contents on other sites in our blog. Besides, Press This bookmarklet, there is one more tool found in the *Tools* page (Figure 7.2). The *Categories and Tags Converter* tool found on the *Tools* page is for converting post categories to tags and vice versa. Recall that we have already used this tool in the previous chapter.

Let us move ahead and see how the content is imported from other blogging platforms. Importing may result in addition of useless content in our blog, therefore it is better to take backup of our blog and also few plugins that are helpful in searching and removing the data that we may not require. The procedure of taking backup of our blog is explained in the next chapter.

7.2 Importing content

On selecting the *Import* option from *Tools* menu, we get a list of importers (refer to Figure 7.6) that we may select for importing contents from blogs on different blogging platforms to our WordPress blog. The importers are packaged in a plugin format, i.e., a plugin is provided for each blogging platform. We have to install and activate the respective plugin to import content from that platform.

 Import

If you have posts or comments in another system, WordPress can import those into this site. To get started, choose a system to import from below:

Blogger	Install the Blogger importer to import posts, comments, and users from a Blogger blog.
Blogroll	Install the blogroll importer to import links in OPML format.
Categories and Tags Converter	Install the category/tag converter to convert existing categories to tags or tags to categories, selectively.
LiveJournal	Install the LiveJournal importer to import posts from LiveJournal using their API.
Movable Type and TypePad	Install the Movable Type importer to import posts and comments from a Movable Type or TypePad blog.
RSS	Install the RSS importer to import posts from an RSS feed.
WordPress	Install the WordPress importer to import posts, pages, comments, custom fields, categories, and tags from a WordPress export file.

If the importer you need is not listed, search the plugins directory to see if an importer is available.

Figure 7.6 List of importers listed in the Import Page

The list of plugins shown in the Import page confirms that we can import contents from multiple blogging platforms. However, to import content from any blogging platform, we can follow some simple steps listed as below:

1. Select the link of the desired blogging platforms from which we want to import content.

2. Install the respective importer plugin.

3. Activate and Run the installed importer plugin.

4. Specify either the file containing the information of the content to import or the authorization information to import content from the specified platform.

Note: Only content migration is possible as settings are not transferred.

Let us look at the process of importing information from each blogging platform individually.

7.2.1 Importing from Blogger

Before we begin our procedure of importing content from the Blogger platform, we need to make sure that we should have a blog at the site, `Blogger.com`. If we do not have a blog at this website we first need to create one before beginning with the steps of importing contents from Blogger.

Follow the steps given below for creating a blog at Blogger.com:

1. Open the site, `Blogger.com` where we are asked to enter our Gmail ID and password. We will need to create a Gmail account in case we do not have one.

2. On entering the valid email ID and password, we get a dialog box that provides several links such as View Profile, Edit Profile, Edit Photo, etc. The dialog box also displays a button, *CREATE YOUR BLOG NOW* that we need to select to create a blog.

3. Next, we are asked to enter a Blog title and Blog address (URL). Let us, for example, enter the Blog title as *Web Development* and Blog address (URL) as http://harwaniweb.blogspot.com (refer to Figure 7.7) followed by selecting the *CONTINUE* button.

Figure 7.7 Specifying Blog title and its URL in Blogger.com

4. Select a starter template to set the layout of the blog. Choose any template and selected the *CONTINUE* button for the next step.

5. Our blog titled *Web Development* is created and is confirmed by the following dialog box that displays a message, *Your blog has been created!*. To add content to the blog, we need to select the *START BLOGGING* link to create a post.

6. We get a dashboard that displays tabs to do several tasks such as publish posts, write comments, change settings, etc. Here, we select the first tab, *Posting* as we are interested in creating content for our blog. On doing this, three links appear below the Posting tab, *New Post, Edit Posts* and *Edit Pages* (refer to Figure 7.9). We now select the *New Post* link to create a new post.

7. Next, we get a page to enter content for the new post. We need to specify title for the new post in the *Title* box (refer to Figure 7.8) and the content of the post in the large box below it. After specifying *Labels* for the new post, we select the *PUBLISH POST* button to publish the post

Figure 7.8 Creating and publishing a post in the blog created in Blogger.com

If the post is successfully published, we get a confirmation message along with a link to view the post as shown in Figure 7.9. We are also provided with the links to edit the post and to create a new post.

[120]

Figure 7.9 Message confirming successful publishing of the post

Now since we have a blog in `Blogger.com`, we can import its content in our WordPress blog. Let us now return to our blog and select the *Tools->Import* option from the main navigation menu to open the *Import* page (Figure 7.6). From the *Import* page, select the link, *Blogger* to install the *Blogger Importer* plugin on our server, which is required to import content from the Blogger platform. On doing this, we get a *Description* page of the *Blogger Importer* plugin displaying the information such as its *Version, Author, Compatibility*, etc. The page also has a *Install Now* button to download, unpack and install the plugin on our server. If the plugin is installed properly, we are informed of the successful installation of the plugin with two links, *Activate Plugin & Run Importer* and *Return to Importers*, where the former link activates the *Blogger Importer* plugin and initiates the process of importing from the *Blogger* platform whereas the latter link takes us to the *Import* page. Let us select the *Activate* Plugin & *Run Importer* link.

On doing this, we get a page informing what type of contents can be imported by the Blogger Importer plugin and what things are needed to use this plugin as shown in Figure 7.10. We are also asked to select the *Authorize* button so as to authorize the WordPress blog to access content on the Blogger platform.

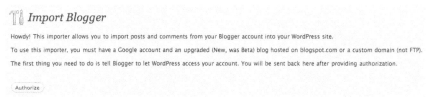

Figure 7.10 Authorizing WordPress to access content on Blogger platform

We are asked to supply our Gmail ID and password. On entering a valid email ID and password, we get a page displaying a message that WordPress blog is requesting access to Google account. Also two buttons, *Grant access* and *Deny access* are displayed as shown in Figure 7.11. *Grant access* allows the WordPress blog to access the contents in the Blogger platform whereas the *Deny access* button cancels the import procedure.

Figure 7.11 Options to grant or deny access to WordPress from accessing the Blogger account

On selecting the *Grant access* button, we get a page displaying information of the blog on the Blogger platform such as the blog title, its URL, number of posts in it, comments, etc. The page also displays an *Import* button that can be selected to begin the import process. All the content is imported to our WordPress blog. The posts are imported with the current user as author. We get a page as shown in Figure 7.12 to map the authors. Since the author(s) of the posts in Blogger's blog might be different from the users in our WordPress blog so, by author mapping, we substitute the name of the original author by the users on our blog. The figure displays the title and URL of the Blogger's blog. On the left-hand side is the original author(s) of the posts of Blogger's blog and from the drop down menu under the WordPress login, we select the author of our blog who is mapped or replaces the original author. When author mapping is done, we save the changes by selecting the *Save Changes* button.

Help ∨

Author mapping

Web Development (harwaniweb.blogspot.com)

All posts were imported with the current user as author. Use this form to move each Blogger user's posts to a different WordPress user. You may add users and then return to this page and complete the user mapping. This form may be used as many times as you like until you activate the "Restart" function below.

Blogger username	WordPress login
B.M.Harwanihttp://www.blogger.com/profile/00248685102390988020noreply@blogger.com	admin ⬍

Save Changes

Restart

We have saved some information about your Blogger account in your WordPress database. Clearing this information will allow you to start over. Restarting will not affect any posts you have already imported. If you attempt to re-import a blog, duplicate posts and comments will be skipped.

Clear account information

Figure 7.12 Mapping authors for the imported posts

7.2.2 Importing from Blogroll

We know that Blogroll refers to a link category that contains several links. To import links from the Blogroll, we select the link *Blogroll* from the *Import* page. Again as expected, a description page gets opened up displaying the information of the plugin, *OPML Importer* that imports the links in OPML format. OPML stands for *Outline Processor Markup Language* and is an XML format for links. The Description page also displays the *Install Now* button that we select to install the plugin. On successful installation of the plugin, we are informed about the same and are prompted to activate the plugin as shown in Figure 7.13.

Installing Plugin: OPML Importer 0.2

Downloading install package from http://downloads.wordpress.org/plugin/opml-importer.zip...

Unpacking the package...

Installing the plugin...

Successfully installed the plugin **OPML Importer 0.2**.

Actions: Activate Plugin & Run Importer | Return to Importers

Figure 7.13 Message confirming successful installation of OPML Importer plugin

On selecting the *Activate Plugin & Run Importer* link, the OPML Importer plugin gets activated and executes to begin the import procedure. We get a page to specify the OPML URL of the blog whose blogroll we want to import (refer to Figure 7.14). Let us assume, we have a WordPress blog with URL http://bintuharwani.wordpress.com and we want to import its blogroll in our current blog bmharwani.com. In WordPress, OPML is already created for us and is accessible through the URL with following format:

```
http://blogURL/wp-links-opml.php
```

Using above URL format, the OPML URL of the blog, http://bintuharwani.wordpress.com will be http://bintuharwani.wordpress.com/wp-links-opml.php. Using this OPML URL we can import its links into our blog. After specifying the OPML URL, we need to specify the link category in our current blog where we want to put the imported links through the *Category* drop down menu. Recall, we have two link categories in our blog, *Blogroll* (default) and *My Articles*. Let us insert the imported links in the default link category, Blogroll. To initiate the import process, we select the button, *Import OPML file*.

Figure 7.14 Page to specify the OPML URL of the blog

On doing this, all the links are imported and we get a confirming message as shown in Figure 7.15.

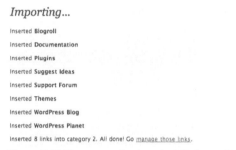

Figure 7.15 Messages displayed while importing links

7.2.3 Importing from LiveJournal

Let us assume that we have a blog in the LiveJournal platform. We can import its content in our WordPress blog by using the following steps:

1. Select the *Tools->Import* option from the main navigation menu to open the *Import* page and select the *LiveJournal* link.

2. A page is opened showing description of the plugin, *LiveJournal Importer* that is required to be installed on our server for importing contents. The *Description* page contains an *Install Now* button that we need to select to install the plugin.

3. On successful installation of the *LiveJournal Importer* plugin, we need to select the *Activate Plugin & Run Importer* link to activate and execute the plugin and to begin the import procedure.

4. We now get an *Import LiveJournal* page prompting us to supply *LiveJournal Username* and *Password* as shown in Figure 7.16. This authentication allows the plugin to connect to our account in LiveJournal and subsequently access the content.

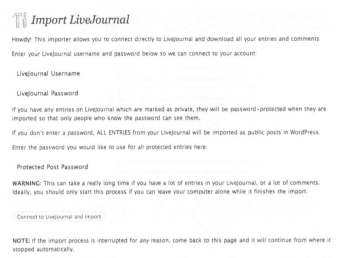

Import LiveJournal

Howdy! This importer allows you to connect directly to LiveJournal and download all your entries and comments

Enter your LiveJournal username and password below so we can connect to your account:

LiveJournal Username

LiveJournal Password

If you have any entries on LiveJournal which are marked as private, they will be password-protected when they are imported so that only people who know the password can see them.

If you don't enter a password, ALL ENTRIES from your LiveJournal will be imported as public posts in WordPress.

Enter the password you would like to use for all protected entries here:

Protected Post Password

WARNING: This can take a really long time if you have a lot of entries in your LiveJournal, or a lot of comments. Ideally, you should only start this process if you can leave your computer alone while it finishes the import.

Connect to LiveJournal and Import

NOTE: If the import process is interrupted for *any* reason, come back to this page and it will continue from where it stopped automatically.

Figure 7.16 Entering Username and Password for accessing the LiveJournal account

After entering a valid LiveJournal Username and Password, we select the *Connect to LiveJournal and Import* button to import the content from the LiveJournal blog into our WordPress blog.

7.2.4 Importing from Movable Type and TypePad

To import the content from the blog that is on Movable Type and TypePad platform, the first thing we need to do is to create an export file containing content of that blog. For the export file, we need to Sign In on the TypePad site. We will have to create an account on TypePad in case we do not have one. On Signing In, we are taken to the Dashboard page that displays several links to manage blog. We can use the links in the Dashboard to do several tasks such as publish posts, write comments, change settings, etc.

An export file can be created through the *Settings* page, so let us now select the *Settings* link from the Dashboard to open it. The *Settings* page contains several tabs that can be used to change the settings of Posts, Categories, Comments, SEO, Import/Export, etc. We select the *Import/Export* tab to see the options of importing and exporting contents from TypePad. A page is displayed as shown in Figure 7.17.

Figure 7.17 Options of Import/Export tab of the Settings page

We can see the Import box displays the options to import contents from different platforms such as TypePad, Movable Type, WordPress or WordPress's WXR file (RSS file). The Export box displays a message informing what the contents are that can be exported through the export procedure. Since, we want an export file, lets select the *Export* button found at the bottom of the *Export* box. On selecting the *Export* button, the contents of the blog are exported and a *Download* link appears in the *Export* box. On selecting the *Download* link, we are asked to specify the name by which we want to save the export file on our computer. Let us specify the name of the export file as *mt-export.txt.*

Note: The export file mt-export.txt contains the content of the blog on TypePad site

Now, since, we have an export file containing the data that we want to import in our WordPress blog, we can go ahead importing the file. Select the *Tools->Import* option from the main navigation menu to open the *Import* page. From the Import page, select the *Movable Type and TypePad* link to install the required plugin. A description page for the plugin, Movable Type and TypePad Importer appears on the screen displaying the information regarding the version, author, compatibility, etc. of the plugin along with an *Install Now* button. On selecting the *Install Now* button the plugin, *Movable Type and TypePad Importer* is installed on our server. A confirmation message appears showing the successful installation of the plugin along with two links, *Activate Plugin & Run Importer* and *Return to importers* where the first link activates the plugin and initiates the import procedure whereas the second link takes us back to the *Import* page. We can now select the *Activate Plugin & Run Importer* link to begin with our task of importing contents.

We get an *Import Movable Type or TypePad* page (refer to Figure 7.18) prompting us to specify the file that we want to import. Use the *Choose File* button to select the file from our computer. Here, we select the *file mt-export.txt* that contains the content of the blog on TypePad we just created through its export procedure. After specifying the file, we select the *Upload file and import* button to import its content in our WordPress blog.

Import Movable Type or TypePad

Howdy! We are about to begin importing all of your Movable Type or TypePad entries into WordPress. To begin, either choose a file to upload and click "Upload file and import", or use FTP to upload your MT export file as mt-export.txt in your /wp-content/ directory and then click "Import mt-export.txt".

Choose a file from your computer: (Maximum size: 64MB) (Choose File) mt-export.txt

Upload file and import

Or use mt-export.txt in your /wp-content/ directory

Import mt-export.txt

The importer is smart enough not to import duplicates, so you can run this multiple times without worry if—for whatever reason—it doesn't finish. If you get an out of memory error try splitting up the import file into pieces.

Figure 7.18 Specifying the file to upload and import

Since the author(s) of the post that is imported may be different from the users on our blog, an *Assign Authors* page opens to assign the author that exists on our blog to the imported post(s) as shown in Figure 7.19. The page is for substituting the original author in the imported posts with the author(s) or users in our blog. We can even create a new user to be assigned to the imported post(s), if desired.

Assign Authors

To make it easier for you to edit and save the imported posts and drafts, you may want to change the name of the author of the posts. For example, you may want to import all the entries as admin's entries.

Below, you can see the names of the authors of the Movable Type posts in *italics*. For each of these names, you can either pick an author in your WordPress installation from the menu, or enter a name for the author in the textbox.

If a new user is created by WordPress, a password will be randomly generated. Manually change the user's details if necessary.

1. Current author: **bmharwani**
   Create user bmharwani
   or map to existing bmharwani ⬧

Submit

Figure 7.19 Assigning authors to the imported content

After assigning the authors to the imported posts, we select the *Submit* button to begin the import process. This way, all the contents of the blog in the TypePad platform are imported in our WordPress blog.

7.2.5 Importing from RSS Feed

We can import posts from other blogs through RSS feeds. Remember, through RSS Importer, we can import only posts and not comments, trackbacks, categories or users. The first thing that we need is to have a RSS 2.0 file that is required at the time of import. The easiest way to create an RSS feed file is to use the export method. That is, open the blog whose RSS feeds we want to import in our WordPress blog and open its *Export* page. The *Export* page (refer to Figure 7.24) may or may not have filters depending on whether the blog is on hosted or self-hosted platform. Filters allow us to export more specific contents. In any case, we need to select the *Download Export File* button to save the export file, which is an xml file containing the blog contents on our computer.

Note: WordPress exports an XML file known as the WordPress eXtended RSS or WXR that contains all of our posts, pages, comments, custom fields, categories and tags. The plugins, themes, and settings are not included in the WXR export file.

Having WXR file in hand, we can go ahead and import RSS feed into our blog.

Now, open our WordPress blog and follow the steps given below to import posts via RSS:

1. Open the Import page by selecting the *Tools->Import page* from the main navigation menu.

2. Select the RSS link from the Import page. A *Description* page displaying information of the *RSS Importer* plugin gets displayed. The RSS Importer plugin can extract posts from any valid RSS 2.0 file or feed into our WordPress blog.

3. Select the *Install Now* button in the *Description* page to install the *RSS Importer* plugin. On doing this, we get a confirmation message of successful installation of RSS Importer.

4. Select the *Activate Plugin & Run Importer* link to activate and execute the plugin. We get *the Import RSS* page asking for the RSS 2.0 file to upload as shown in Figure 7.20.

Figure 7.20 Uploading and importing file to extract posts

5. Select *Choose file* button to get the list of files in our computer. After selecting the file that we saved earlier using the export method, select the *Upload file and import* button to initiate the process of importing posts from RSS feeds. The posts will be imported and we get the confirming message as shown in Figure 7.21.

Figure 7.21 Message displayed while importing posts through RSS

Let us assume, we have a WordPress blog with URL `http://bintuharwani.wordpress.com` and we want to import its contents into our current WordPress blog, `bmharwani.com`. For this, we have to first open the `bintuharwani.wordpress.com` blog and export its content. To export a blog, we have to open its *Export Page* by selecting the *Tools->Export* option from the main navigation menu. From the Export page, select *Download Export File* button to save the export file (WXR file) on our computer. Then, we open the blog, `bmharwani.com`, where we want to import the contents. Open its Import page and after installing the *RSS Importer* plugin, we specify the export file of `bmharwani.wordpress.com` blog and select *Upload and import* button to import the contents of the WXR file into our blog..

7.2.6 Importing from WordPress platform

To import content from a WordPress blog, first we need to export its contents into a file. As discussed in the previous section, we can use the Export page to create an export file, i.e., an XML file containing the content of the blog.

Note: The maximum allowable file size that can be imported is 15MB. In case, we have a file that is larger than 15MB in size, we split it into smaller files and import them separately.

Once, we have the export file, we can import its contents in our blog by following the below given simple steps:

1. Open the Import page by selecting the *Tools->Import* page from the main navigation menu.

2. Out of the list of importers displayed in the *Import* page, select the *WordPress* link. A *Description* page displaying information of the *WordPress Importer* plugin gets displayed. The *WordPress Importer* plugin can extract posts, pages, comment, custom fields, categories and tags from a WordPress export file (WXR file) into our WordPress blog.

3. Select the *Install Now* button in the *Description* page to install the *WordPress Importer* plugin. We get a confirming message of successful installation of WordPress Importer.

4. Select the *Activate Plugin & Run Importer* link to activate and execute the plugin. We get *Import WordPress* page asking for the WXR file to upload as shown in figure 7.22. Here, we will upload the XML file containing exported content of the blog, `bintuharwani.wordpress.com`. Select the *Choose File* button to see the list of files on our computer. Select the WXR file containing the blog contents followed by selecting the *Upload file and import button*

Figure 7.22 Uploading and importing XML file that contains exported content

5. WordPress asks to map the authors of the posts of the imported blog to the authors or users in current blog as shown in Figure 7.23. We can even create a new user to map the author of the imported posts. We check the *Download and import file attachments* checkbox under the *Import Attachments* heading if we want to import the media files from the imported blog. Finally, select the *Submit* button to begin the import procedure. On doing this, all the blog content is imported and a confirmation message is displayed.

Figure 7.23 Assigning authors to the imported content

This is how, we import the contents from different blogging platforms into our WordPress blog. Lets now see how our blog contents can be exported.

7.3 Exporting Content

To export content from our WordPress blog, we select the *Tools -> Export* option from the main navigation menu. WordPress exports an XML file known as the *WordPress eXtended RSS* or WXR that contains all of our posts, pages, comments, custom fields, categories and tags.

Note: The plugins, themes and settings are not included in the WXR export file.

We are provided with several filters in the form of drop down menu to filter the export by date range, author, category, tag, content type and status as shown in Figure 7.24. The *Content Types* drop down allows us to export Posts, Pages or both types of content. Similarly, the *Statuses* drop down menu allows us to export the content in any of the following states: *published, scheduled, draft, pending* or *private* state. These filters not only help in exporting only the specific contents but also in splitting a large blog into several pieces.

Export

When you click the button below WordPress will create an XML file for you to save to your computer.

This format, which we call WordPress eXtended RSS or WXR, will contain your posts, pages, comments, custom fields, categories, and tags.

Once you've saved the download file, you can use the Import function on another WordPress site to import this site.

Filters

Start Date	All Dates ↕
End Date	All Dates ↕
Authors	All Authors ↕
Categories	All Terms ↕
Post Tags	All Terms ↕
Content Types	All Content ↕
Statuses	All Statuses ↕

Download Export File

Figure 7.24 Filters in Export Page

Let us now see how settings of the WordPress blog can be modified.

7.4 Settings

The Settings menu is used to control several aspects of our site. On selecting the Settings menu from the main navigation menu, we get the menu options as shown in Figure 7.25.

Note: Several plugins add more menu options to the Settings menu.

Settings

General
Writing
Reading
Discussion
Media
Privacy
Permalinks

Figure 7.25 Options in the Settings menu

7.4.1 General Settings

Through General Settings we can control the appearance of our blog. For example, we can set the title of the blog, tag line displayed in the header of the blog, email address of the administrator, default role of the new user joining the blog, time zone, date format, etc. On selecting the *Settings->General* option from the main navigation menu, we get the list of options as shown in Figure 7.26.

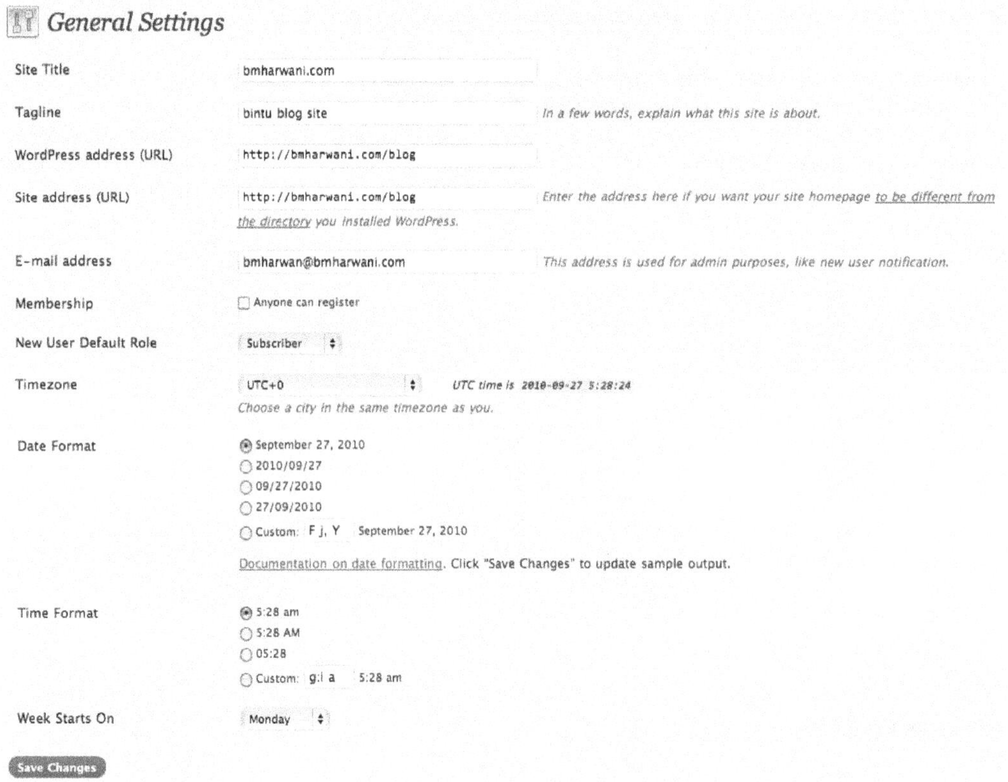

General Settings

Site Title	bmharwani.com	
Tagline	bintu blog site	In a few words, explain what this site is about.
WordPress address (URL)	http://bmharwani.com/blog	
Site address (URL)	http://bmharwani.com/blog	Enter the address here if you want your site homepage to be different from
	the directory you installed WordPress.	
E-mail address	bmharwan@bmharwani.com	This address is used for admin purposes, like new user notification.
Membership	☐ Anyone can register	
New User Default Role	Subscriber ⬍	
Timezone	UTC+0 ⬍ UTC time is 2010-09-27 5:28:24	
	Choose a city in the same timezone as you.	
Date Format	⦿ September 27, 2010	
	◯ 2010/09/27	
	◯ 09/27/2010	
	◯ 27/09/2010	
	◯ Custom: F j, Y September 27, 2010	
	Documentation on date formatting. Click "Save Changes" to update sample output.	
Time Format	⦿ 5:28 am	
	◯ 5:28 AM	
	◯ 05:28	
	◯ Custom: g:i a 5:28 am	
Week Starts On	Monday ⬍	

Save Changes

Figure 7.26 General Settings page

The *Site Title* box displays the blog name or blog title that we had entered during the installation of WordPress. We can change it to any text that we want to appear at the top of every page. In the Tagline box, we enter a brief description of our site that may be displayed near the blog title, depending on the applied theme. In the *WordPress address (URL)* box, we enter the full URL of the directory where WordPress is installed. For example, if our domain name is bmharwani.com and we have installed WordPress in the root directory, then the WordPress address URL will be http://bmharwani.com. In case, the WordPress is installed in a separate directory named *blog*, then the WordPress address URL will be http://bmharwani.com/blog

In the *Site address (URL)* box, we enter the address through which our blog will be accessed. It is the directory where WordPress's main *index.php* file is installed and is usually the same as WordPress address (URL). In the *E-mail address* box, we enter the email address of the administrator who will receive notifications when either a new user registers to our blog or when a comment is submitted for moderation, etc.

The next option, *Membership* decides whether we want any user to register at our blog or not. Let us have a look at it.

Allowing users to register

The *Membership* option of *General Settings* decides whether we want visitors to register at our blog or not. We can check the checkbox *Anyone can register* to allow anyone to register at our blog. The *Meta Widget* if displayed in sidebars usually appears as shown in Figure 7.27(a) displaying links used for doing tasks such as administering the blog, logging in and out of the blog, accessing RSS feeds and WordPress site. When the checkbox, *Anyone can register* is checked, we find that one extra link, *Register* is added to the *Meta Widget* as shown in Figure 7.27(b).

Figure 7.27 (a) Usual links in Meta Widget (b) Register link appears among links of Meta Widget

On selecting the *Register* link, we get a Login page asking for a valid Username and Password as shown in Figure 7.28(a). Below the box, we can find a link, *Register* that is meant for the new user to select to get the Registration page. On selecting the *Register* link, we get a Registration page asking for the *Username* and *E-mail* address of the new user as shown in Figure 7.28(b). After entering the user name and email address in the respective boxes, we need to select the *Register* button to create a new account. On selecting the *Register* button, we get a message, '*Registration complete. Please check your e-mail*'.

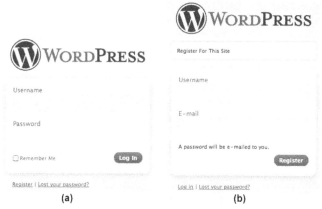

Figure 7.28 (a) Log in page showing Register link at bottom (b) Page asking information for new user

Why the Registration page asks only for *Username* and *Email* address? This is because the rest of the information of the new user such as their *First Name, Last Name, Nickname, Website, Biographical Info*, etc. can be entered later through the *Profile* page. After entering the *Username* and *Email* address, when user selects the *Register* button, the account for the new user is created and a password to access the account is mailed to them along with a link to login into the blog as shown in Figure 7.29(a). Besides this, an email is sent to the administrator to inform about the new registration as shown in Figure 7.29(b).

Figure 7.29 (a) Email containing password information of the new user (b) Email received by the administrator informing of the new user

The default role of the new user is *Subscriber*. Recall that we have already learnt about different pre-defined roles of WordPress in Chapter 5.

The *New User Default Role* drop down menu in *General Settings* helps us in deciding the default role of the newly registered user. The drop down menu displays five options to choose from, Subscriber, Contributor, Author, Editor and Administrator.

Note: The role of user can be later changed through the Users page.

Timezone

Timezone drop down allows us to select UTC (Universal Coordinated Time) timezone or the city that is in our current timezone. If we select a city in our timezone, then we do not have to change it again to account for Daylight Saving Time. WordPress.com automatically updates our blog's time settings as needed.

Daylight Saving Time (DST) also known as summer time in many countries is the practice of temporarily advancing clocks during the summer time so that afternoons have more daylight and mornings have less. Typically clocks are adjusted forward one hour near the start of spring and are adjusted backward in autumn. The idea behind doing so is to make better use of the daylight in the evenings that helps in reducing road accidents, gives more time to children to play and spend with friends and family, etc.

Setting Date and Time format

The Date Format option of *General Settings* displays several formats of dates to choose from. We can even create our own custom date format by entering specific format characters in the *Custom* box. The list of format characters that are used for creating custom date are shown in Table 7.1.

Table 7.1 Brief description of format characters for custom date format

Format character	Usage
d	Displays days in numeric with leading zeros. Example, 01–31
j	Displays days in numeric without leading zeros. Example, 1–31
S	Used after j character to apply English ordinal suffix such as st, nd, rd or th. Example, 23rd, 10th
m	Displays month in numeric with leading zeros. Example, 01–12
n	Displays month in numeric without leading zeros. Example, 1–12
F	Displays month in full Textual format. Example, January – December
M	Displays first three letters of the month. Example, Jan – Dec
Y	Displays year in 4 numeric digits. Example, 2010
y	Displays year in 2 numeric digits. Example, 10

The *Time Format* option of *General Settings* displays several formats of time to choose from. Through time format, we can create our own custom time format by entering specific format characters in the *Custom* box. The list of format characters that are used for creating custom time are shown in Table 7.2.

Table 7.2 Brief description of format characters for custom time format

Format character	Usage
l	Displays full name for day of the week. Example, Sunday, Monday
D	Displays first three letters for day of the week. Example, Sun, Mon

Format character	Usage
a	Displays am, pm (in lowercase).
A	Displays AM, PM (in uppercase).
g	Displays hour in 12-hour format without leading zeros. Example, 1–12
h	Displays hour in 12-hour format with leading zeros. Example, 01–12
G	Displays hour in 24-hour format without leading zeros. Example, 0-23
H	Displays hour in 24-hour format with leading zeros. Example, 00-23
i	Displays minutes with leading zeros. Example, 00-59
s	Displays seconds, with leading zeros. Example, 00-59
T	Displays Timezone abbreviation. Example, EST, MDT
c	Displays full date and time in ISO 8601 format. Example, 2010-11-29T16:20:15+00:00
r	Displays full date and time in RFC 2822 format. Example, Mon, 29 Nov 2010 4:20:15 + 0000

Examples:
- m-d-Y displays date as 05-09-2010
- jS F, Y displays 9th May, 2010
- jS F,Y g:i a displays 9th May, 2010 12:15 pm
- jS F,Y g:i a T displays 9th May, 2010 12:15 pm GMT

The final option of the *General Settings*, the *Week Starts On* decides which day begins the week in the calendar. That is, which day of a week(Sun, Mon…) should be displayed in the first column of the calendar. As is obvious, we can see the impact of using this option while displaying calendar in the sidebars using the Calendar Widget.

7.4.2 Writing Settings

The Writings Settings helps us in configuring user interface and enhancing writing experience. It displays several options that help us in doing several tasks such as determining the default size of the post box, defining default post and link categories, publishing posts via email, enabling remote publishing and defining sites to ping when new content is published on our site. To open the Writing Settings page, we select the *Settings->Writing* option from the main navigation menu. The page opens up displaying options as shown in Figure 7.30.

⚙ Writing Settings

Size of the post box	10 lines

Formatting	☑ Convert emoticons like :-) and :-P to graphics on display
	☐ WordPress should correct invalidly nested XHTML automatically

Default Post Category	General ⬍

Default Link Category	Blogroll ⬍

Press This

Press This is a bookmarklet: a little app that runs in your browser and lets you grab bits of the web.

Use Press This to clip text, images and videos from any web page. Then edit and add more straight from Press This before you save or publish it in a post on your site.

Drag-and-drop the following link to your bookmarks bar or right click it and add it to your favorites for a posting shortcut.

Press This

Post via e-mail

To post to WordPress by e-mail you must set up a secret e-mail account with POP3 access. Any mail received at this address will be posted, so it's a good idea to keep this address very secret. Here are three random strings you could use: YGNjqEdu , Ge2jA9kf , eLE6201J .

Mail Server	mail.bmharwani.com	Port	110
Login Name	pqr123@bmharwani.com		
Password			
Default Mail Category	General ⬍		

Remote Publishing

To post to WordPress from a desktop blogging client or remote website that uses the Atom Publishing Protocol or one of the XML-RPC publishing interfaces you must enable them below.

Atom Publishing Protocol	☐ Enable the Atom Publishing Protocol.
XML-RPC	☐ Enable the WordPress, Movable Type, MetaWeblog and Blogger XML-RPC publishing protocols.

Update Services

When you publish a new post, WordPress automatically notifies the following site update services. For more about this, see Update Services on the Codex. Separate multiple service URLs with line breaks.

```
http://rpc.pingomatic.com/
```

Save Changes

Figure 7.30 Writing Settings Page

The *Size* of the post box is used to determine the default size of the post box and the page edit box. The size of the post box can also be changed by dragging its lower right corner. If the post is of size larger then the size specified; a scroll box appears for this in the post box. From the Formatting option, we check the checkbox, *Convert emoticons like :-) and :-P to graphics on display* to convert all of the emoticons in our posts into graphical smilies. The checkbox, *WordPress should correct invalidly nested XHTML automatically* is checked to make sure that the XHTML code written in any posts is a valid code. The *Default Post Category* drop down menu is for specifying the default category for the posts. We know that the posts have to be assigned to at least one category. Let us select the *General* category as the default category for the new posts. Recall, that we changed the name of the default category, *Uncategorized* to *General* in Chapter 2. Similarly, the *Default Link Category* drop down menu is for specifying the default link category for the new links. Recall, like posts, the links also have to be assigned to at least one link category.

Let us select the default link category, *Blogroll* from this drop down menu. The *Press This* link works in the same way that we have seen and used in *Tools* menu. We can also submit posts to our blog through email. Let us see how.

Submitting posts via email

The *Post via e-mail option* of *Writing Settings* allows us to submit our post via email. For this, we need to create a new e-mail account on our web host's mail server. The mail server receives e-mails and stores them for future use. For that, we need to specify information for the following:

- **Mail Server**—Enter the URI address of the web host's mail server. It is provided by the web hosting service provider. Let us assume the URI address of my mail server is `mail.bmharwani.com`

  Note: Do not use public, free e-mail servers such as Yahoo, Hotmail, etc. for this account.

- **Port**—Servers usually use port *110* to receive requests related to emails. Confirm it with your web hosting service provider

- **Login Name**—Enter the email address of the account that we created on our web host's mail server. Its better to have a random string (hard to guess) for the account name. Assuming the name by which we created account on our web host's mail server is *pqr123*, hence the login name will be *pqr123@bmharwani.com*

- **Password**—Enter the password for the e-mail address we entered in the *Login Name* box. Since the password appears as a plain text, I have deliberately erased the password from the Figure 7.30.

- **Default Mail Category**—Select the category to which we want to assign the mailed post. Let us select the default category, *General* here.

Setting up WordPress to publish the email messages

Now, from any email account, we can send a mail to the account, `pqr123@bmharwani.com` containing the post that we want to submit to our blog. The post sent by mail will not appear on our blog until we setup WordPress to publish those email messages on our blog. To set up WordPress to publish the email messages to our blog, we need to go to the URL with following syntax:

`http://domain_name/installation_directory/wp-mail.php`

Considering the domain of our blog is `bmharwani.com` and the directory where WordPress is installed is *blog*, the link for us is as follows:

`http://bmharwani.com/blog/wp-mail.php`

Note: We have to go to above said URL after every mail that we send to publish our post.

On pointing the browser to the above said URL, our post gets published and the mail deleted from our mail account. We might get the messages as shown in Figure 7.31. The figure displays the email sender's name as the author of the post titled, 'How to use Functions in PHP'.

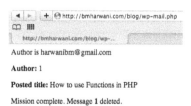

Author is harwanibm@gmail.com

Author: 1

Posted title: How to use Functions in PHP

Mission complete. Message 1 deleted.

Figure 7.31 Publishing the posts sent by mail and deleting them from the mailbox

In our *Posts* page, we find the mailed post with *Pending* status. To publish it to our blog, we need to change its status to *Published* state. To change the status of the post, we hover over its title and select the *Edit* link out of the four links, *Edit, Quick Edit, Trash* and *View* that appears below the title. When the post is opened in the edit mode, we select the *Publish* button to publish it on the blog. The post is published and assigned to the category that we specified in the *Default Mail Category* drop down menu. To assign the mailed post to some other category, our e-mail subject should begin with *[n]*, where *n* is the *ID* of the category to which we want to assign the mailed post.

If we send a mail containing content of the post through Yahoo! Mail, Gmail or Hotmail, we find that the body of the post is missing. It is so as most of the web-based email clients send messages in HTML format and HTML tags are automatically filtered out by the blog by the email feature. So, the solution for sending the body of the post is to send the post content in *plain text* form. In Yahoo! Mail, the link, *Plain Text* found below the *Subject* field converts the matter to plain text. The same job is done in Gmail by a link, *Plain Text* located at the right end of the text formatting tool bar. In Hotmail, we find a similar link next to the *Spell Check* button in the email action bar found above the email message.

Remote Publishing

In order to post from a desktop client, or remote website, we need to enable either the Atom or the XML-RPC protocol. There are several desktop clients available such as *MarsEdit, BlogDesk, Windows Live Writer* and many more. Desktop clients allow us to write and save posts while offline and publish them to our blog when we are connected to the internet.

To explain posting from a desktop client, I have used *Qumana* in this book. *Qumana* is an easy-to-use desktop blog editor that enables us to write, edit and post to one or more blogs. Again, Qumana can be used when we are offline. We can write and save posts and can upload them to our blog whenever we are online. Qumana has a WYSIWYG editor, easy-to-understand buttons, spell check facility and much more. It is available for Windows, Mac and Linux platforms. It can be downloaded from the following URL, `http://www.qumana.com/`

Steps to post through Qumana

1. On executing Qumana, the first screen we get is a Welcome message. Select the OK button to move further. We will be prompted to specify the URL of the blog.

2. After entering the URL, select the Next button.

3. Enter the login information of the administrator. After entering username and password required to access the blog, select the Next button.

4. The list of blogs present in the specified URL is listed. Select the blog that we are interested in adding to Qumana followed by the Finish button.

5. All the posts that are present in the selected blog are accessed and displayed in the Qumana Blog Manager as shown in Figure 7.32. As expected, the only post in our blog, *Working with Forms* appears.

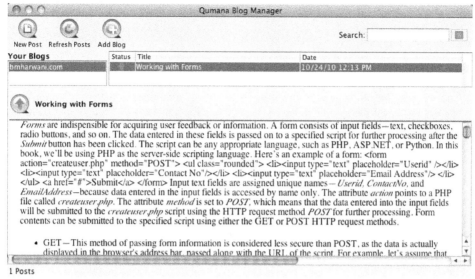

Figure 7.32 Post displayed in Qumana Blog Manager

6. Select the *New Post* icon from the *Blog Manager* to write a new post. Let us assume that the title of the new post is *Converting Lowercase to Uppercase through AJAX*. After entering content of the new post, we need to select the category to which we want to assign the post. The two categories of our blog, *General* and *Smartphone Articles* are listed. Let us select the *Smartphone Articles* category for the new post as shown in Figure 7.33.

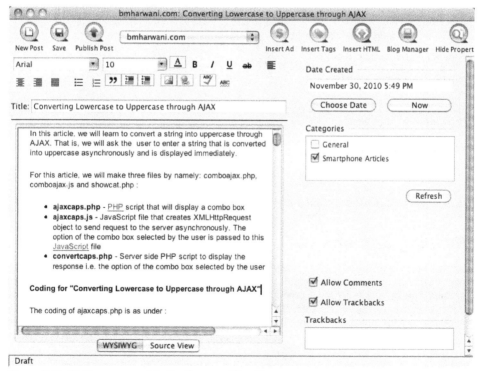

Figure 7.33 Writing new post in the Qumana Blog Manager

7. Select either the *Save* icon to save the draft or the *Publish Post* icon to publish the post to the blog.

Update Services

Update Services displays a box where we can enter a list of ping services. Ping services are those sites that aggregate information about the blogs that are recently updated and inform the visitors about the updated contents. That is, they let other people know when we have updated our blog's content. A ping service, *Ping-o-matic* is automatically listed in the box. It is a central site that feeds into lots of other services. We can add more ping services to this box.

There is a very long list of ping services. Few of them are listed below:

- http://api.moreover.com/RPC2
- http://bblog.com/ping.php
- http://blogsearch.google.com/ping/RPC2
- http://ping.weblogalot.com/rpc.php
- http://ping.feedburner.com
- http://ping.syndic8.com/xmlrpc.php
- http://ping.bloggers.jp/rpc/
- http://rpc.pingomatic.com/
- http://rpc.weblogs.com/RPC2
- http://rpc.technorati.com/rpc/ping
- http://topicexchange.com/RPC2
- http://www.blogpeople.net/servlet/weblogUpdates
- http://xping.pubsub.com/ping
- http://api.moreover.com/RPC2
- http://api.my.yahoo.com/RPC2
- http://audiorpc.weblogs.com/RPC2
- http://blogpeople.net/ping
- http://blog.goo.ne.jp/XMLRPC

WordPress uses the XML-RPC protocol to ping these sites every time we submit a post.

7.4.3 Reading Settings

The Reading Settings helps in configuring several things that directly impact the initial content that visitor will read or see on opening the blog. For example, we can configure the initial content displayed on the front page of the blog, the default number of posts and feeds displayed, whether to display complete or just the summary of the article in the feeds, etc. To open the Reading Settings page, we select the *Settings->Reading* option from the main navigation menu. We get the list of options as shown in Figure 7.34.

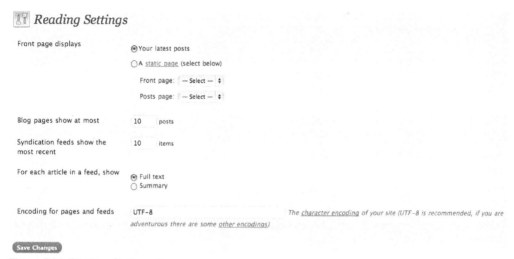

Reading Settings

Front page displays
- ⦿ Your latest posts
- ◯ A static page (select below)

  Front page: — Select — ⇕
  Posts page: — Select — ⇕

Blog pages show at most `10` posts

Syndication feeds show the most recent `10` items

For each article in a feed, show
- ⦿ Full text
- ◯ Summary

Encoding for pages and feeds `UTF-8` The character encoding of your site (UTF-8 is recommended, if you are adventurous there are some other encodings)

Save Changes

Figure 7.34 Reading Settings Page

The *Front page displays* option allows us to determine what we want to display, the latest posts on the front page of our blog or some static page. The radio button, *Your latest posts* is found selected by default and is meant for displaying latest posts on the front page. The *static page* option is preferred where we do not wish to give a blog-like appearance to our site. For using this option, we need to create two pages, one to act as a splash page displaying information related to introduction, services offered by our organization etc. and the other to display the posts of our site.

We can follow the below given steps to display static page content:

1. Select the *Pages->Add New* option from the main navigation menu to create a new page.

2. Assign the page title as *Home* (or any other name).

3. In the body of the page, enter the introduction of the organization, services offered, etc. and the information that we want should appear on the front page of our blog. We can also insert images, video and audio in this page.

4. Publish the *Home* page

5. Again, select the *Add New* button to create another page

6. Assign the page title as *Posts* (any). Do not write anything in the body of this page as it will be ignored

7. Publish the *Posts* page.

8. Go back to the *Reading Settings* page and from the *Front page displays* heading, select *the A static page (select below)* option. Also, from the *Front page:* drop down menu select the first page, *Home* page and from the *Posts page:* drop down menu, select the second page that we created, i.e., the *Posts* page

9. Save the changes made in the *Reading Settings* page by selecting the *Save Changes* button.

The front page contents of our blog is changed. Now, when a visitor visits our blog instead of latest posts, they will be welcomed with the content that we wrote in the *Home* page. To see the *Posts* of the blog, visitors can select the link, *Posts* that appears in the blog's menu. The *Posts* link might not appear automatically in certain themes. To make the *Posts* link to appear in our blog's menu, we take the help of custom menus. From the main navigation menu select the *Appearance->Menus* option to open the *Menus* Page. In the *Menus* Page, we will find the *Posts* page that we created through above steps in the *Pages* section. Just selects the checkbox of *Posts* page and select the *Add to Menu* button to add its link in the active menu. Refer to Menus section in Chapter 4 for more details.

Note: If we do not specify any page through the *Posts page:* drop down menu (Figure 7.34), then the *Posts* link will not appear in the blog and visitors will be compelled to use indirect approach to access our posts. That is, they will need to use categories links, archive links, etc. to access our posts.

The rest of the options of the *Reading Settings* page are very easy to follow. Their usage is as given as follows:

- **Blog pages show at most**—It determines the number of posts to appear on the blog's front page, archive pages and search results.

- **Syndication feeds show the most recent**—It determines the number of posts to appear in our Atom and RSS feeds.

- **For each article in a feed**—It helps in determining if we want to display the complete text or just a summary of each post (article) to our feed.

- **Encoding for pages and feeds UTF-8**—Here, we enter the character encoding that suits the language that we have chosen for our blog. The default and the safe option is *UTF-8* as this encoding is not only the most commonly accepted character encoding but also supports a wide variety of languages. In case, we import content that uses different character encoding, we can specify that in this box.

7.4.4 Discussion Settings

The Discussion Settings allows us to configure article and comment settings. For example, whether to send notifications or not when anybody links to our article or whether to allow visitors to post comments on articles or not. For comments, the Discussion Settings displays options that decides whether to moderate comments or not, send email when a comment is posted, blacklist sites containing specific content, display commenter's Avatar and so on. The *Discussion Settings* page (refer to Figure 7.35) appears on selecting the *Settings->Discussion* option from the main navigation menu.

Default Article Settings: There are three options to specify the default settings of the article.

- **Attempt to notify any blogs linked to from the article**—If it is checked, WordPress will check if any of our post or page contains links to other blogs. On finding a link to any bog, the blog will be pinged.

- **Allow link notifications from other blogs (pingbacks and trackbacks)** —If it is checked, our blog will be pinged, i.e., we will get a notification if any other blogger links to any content of our blog. Refer to Trackbacks and Pings section of Chapter 3 for more details.

- **Allow people to post comment on new articles**—It determines whether we want the visitors to post their comments on new posts and pages.

Other Comment Settings: Displays several options such as defining pre-requisite condition for the commenter for posting comments, closing comment thread after specific days, enabling nesting in comments, splitting comments in pages, determining display order of comments and so on. The list of options in this section are as follows:

- **Comment author must fill out name and e-mail**—If it is checked, it asks the commenter to provide name and e-mail address for posting comment. If the checkbox is unchecked, we will only have the commenter's IP address.

- **Users must be registered and logged in to comment**—If it is checked, the commenter has to first register and log in to our blog to post comment. This option is preferred while building a community site.

- **Automatically close comments on articles older than n days**—If it is checked, it will make WordPress to automatically close the comment threads on older posts. We need to specify the number of days after which we want to close comments on articles

- **Enable threaded (nested) comments n levels deep**—Threaded or nested comments are very useful as they allow the visitors to comment on our posts as well as on other's comments. In a nested comment list, replies to individual comments are shown indented underneath. We need to specify how many levels deep we want the comments to be nested.

- **Break comments into pages with n top level comments per page and the first/last pages displayed by default**—This option is very useful for handling large number of comments as it splits the comments into pages. We specify the number of top level comments we want per page and also decide which page, *first* or *last* to be displayed by default. The drop down displays two options, *first* and *last* where *first* option refers to the oldest comments and *last* option refers to the latest comments. When the comments are split in pages, navigation links automatically appear allowing us to move from one page to another.

Note: The nested comments are not counted and will not split between two pages.

- **Comments should be displayed with the older/newer comments at the top of each page**—Instead of displaying comments in their original chronological order, we might select this option to display the newest or oldest comments to appear first. The drop down menu displays two options, *older* and *newer* hence allowing us to show the oldest or newest comments, respectively.

E-mail me whenever: This option defines the situations when administrator is to be informed through mail. It displays two checkboxes:

- **Anyone posts a comment**—If it is checked, the author will be informed via mail when anybody comments on her post(s).

- **A comment is held for moderation**—If it is checked, the administrator will receive a mail informing about the comment awaiting moderation.

Before a comment appears: It specifies the conditions that must be fulfilled before a comment appears on the site; it displays two checkboxes:

- **An administrator must always approve the comment**—If it is checked then all the comments will be held for moderation and until and unless the administrator approves them, they will not appear on the site. Recall, moderation of comments means that the comments will not appear on the site on submission but will be saved in a queue for the administrator to approve.

- **Comment author must have a previously approved comment**—If it is checked, the comment of the author will be immediately published on the site (without holding it for moderation) if any of author's previous comment is approved.

Comment Moderation: It determines the types of comments that will be held for moderation. That is, they will not be published on the site until the administrator approves them. Since spam comments contain long lists of links, we can specify the upper limit on the number of links that are permissible in a comment. Any comment having that number of links or more will be held for moderation. Besides this, we can specify the list of words, URLs, e-mails and IP addresses, etc. that if found in any comment will also be held for moderation.

Comment Blacklist: We specify the words, names, URLs, e-mails, IP addresses, etc. that if appears in the comment will mark it as black listed, i.e., it will be declared as a spam and hence will not be published.

Avatars: Avatars are little user images that we find along side the comments. Since, few themes do not support Avatars, depending on the current active theme in our blog, the Avatar may or may not appear on our blog. WordPress uses Gravatars (`gravatars.com`), from where people can choose Avatars to be associated with their comments.

Avatar Display: It is used to determine whether to display an Avatar or not. It displays two radio buttons, *Don't show Avatars* and *Show Avatars*. We can select either button depending on whether we want to display Avatars or not.

Maximum Rating: It is used for deciding the maximum rating of the Gravatars that are allowed on our blog. Gravatars include content ratings as shown below:

- **G**—Suitable for all audiences,
- **PG**—Suitable for audiences over 13 and above,
- **R**—Suitable for audiences over 17, and
- **X**—Suitable for more matured audiences.

By default, only G-rated Gravatars are allowed on a blog

Default Avatar: Used to specify an Avatar for the users who do not have their own custom Avatar on the basis of their email address. Several options are displayed as follows:

- **Mystery Man**—Displays the image of the Mystery Man along side the comment.
- **Blank**—Displays no image of the commenter.
- **Gravatar Logo**—Displays the Gravatar Logo along side the comment.
- **Identicon**—Identicons are computer-generated geometric patterns. A unique pattern will be assigned to each commenter's e-mail address, so that the same pattern is used every time they comment.
- **Wavatar**—Wavatar assembles avatar images with different pieces such as faces, eyes, noses, hair, etc.
- **MonsterID**—MonsterID draws images of monsters instead of geometric designs.

📋 Discussion Settings

Default article settings
- ☑ Attempt to notify any blogs linked to from the article.
- ☑ Allow link notifications from other blogs (pingbacks and trackbacks.)
- ☑ Allow people to post comments on new articles

(These settings may be overridden for individual articles.)

Other comment settings
- ☑ Comment author must fill out name and e-mail
- ☐ Users must be registered and logged in to comment
- ☐ Automatically close comments on articles older than `14` days
- ☑ Enable threaded (nested) comments `5 ♦` levels deep
- ☐ Break comments into pages with `50` top level comments per page and the `last ♦` page displayed by default

Comments should be displayed with the `older ♦` comments at the top of each page

E-mail me whenever
- ☑ Anyone posts a comment
- ☑ A comment is held for moderation

Before a comment appears
- ☐ An administrator must always approve the comment
- ☑ Comment author must have a previously approved comment

Comment Moderation

Hold a comment in the queue if it contains `2` or more links. (A common characteristic of comment spam is a large number of hyperlinks.)

When a comment contains any of these words in its content, name, URL, e-mail, or IP, it will be held in the <u>moderation queue</u>. One word or IP per line. It will match inside words, so "press" will match "WordPress".

Comment Blacklist

When a comment contains any of these words in its content, name, URL, e-mail, or IP, it will be marked as spam. One word or IP per line. It will match inside words, so "press" will match "WordPress".

Avatars

An avatar is an image that follows you from weblog to weblog appearing beside your name when you comment on avatar enabled sites. Here you can enable the disp of avatars for people who comment on your site.

Avatar Display
- ○ Don't show Avatars
- ◉ Show Avatars

Maximum Rating
- ◉ G — Suitable for all audiences
- ○ PG — Possibly offensive, usually for audiences 13 and above
- ○ R — Intended for adult audiences above 17
- ○ X — Even more mature than above

Default Avatar

For users without a custom avatar of their own, you can either display a generic logo or a generated one based on their e-mail address.
- ◉ Mystery Man
- ○ Blank
- ○ Gravatar Logo
- ○ Identicon (Generated)
- ○ Wavatar (Generated)
- ○ MonsterID (Generated)

`Save Changes`

Figure 7.35 Discussion Settings Page

[143]

7.4.5 Media Settings

The Media Settings screen helps in determining the maximum dimensions of the uploaded images and videos. When an image is uploaded for the purpose of embedding in our posts and pages, then besides the original size, WordPress generates it in three different sizes, *thumbnail, medium and large*. So, in all, we have a total of four image sizes for each uploaded image. The idea is to give liberty to the users to choose the image size that best suits their needs. To open the Media Settings page, select the *Settings->Media* option from the main navigation menu. The Media Settings page opens as shown in Figure 7.36.

Figure 7.36 Media Settings Page

Image Sizes: Used to define image sizes for the following:

- **Thumbnail size**—Used to specify the maximum width and height of a thumbnail size image. The default size for thumbnails is 150-pixel square. The checkbox, *Crop thumbnail to exact dimensions* if checked crops the thumbnail to the exact specified size. If the checkbox is unchecked, the image is resized based on the proportional width and height of the original image. Cropping to exact sizes usually results in loosing some part of the image.

- **Medium size**—Used to specify the size of a medium size image. The default size for medium sized image is 300-pixel square.

- **Large size**—Used to specify the size of a large size image. The default size for large sized image is 1024-pixel square.

These default dimensions are usually adequate for most images.

Note: WordPress can reduce the size of the original image to fit in the size specified for thumbnail, medium and large size but cannot enlarge it. For example, if the original image size is say 400 by 400 pixels, then it will be reduced to the thumbnail and medium size but will not be enlarged to the large size dimensions.

Embeds: Displays options to enable/disable the auto-embedding feature of WordPress and to define the maximum allowable dimensions of the embedded media. Its options are

- **Auto-embeds**—In a WordPress blog, we can easily embed videos, images, and other media. For example, to embed video, all we have to do is to put the URL of the video in the post or page and check the checkbox, *Attempt to automatically embed all plain text URLs*. Make sure the URL of the video is in plain text and is not hyperlinked. The WordPress automatically detects the URL and wraps the correct HTML embed code around that URL to make sure the video player is displayed in the post or page. Recall, we have learned the process of embedding video in a post or page in Chapter 2.

- **Maximum embed size**—Enter the maximum width and height of the embedded media. If the width value is left blank, embeds defaults to the maximum width of the currently active theme.

Uploading Files: Used to specify and edit the location of the uploaded media files while writing posts or pages. The following options are displayed using this:

- **Store uploads in this folder**—Used to specify the folder to keep uploaded files. Default path *is wp-content/uploads* folder. The path has to be entered relative to the WordPress installation directory.

- **Full URL path to files**—Enter a URL path for the uploaded files. If this directory does not exist, WordPress creates it while uploading the first media. Alternatively, we can also manually create the directory and make it writeable.

- **Organize my uploads into month-and-year-based folders**—Checking this checkbox makes WordPress to create date-based subdirectories for our uploaded files. That is, subdirectories are created for each year, and within them, sub-sub directories are also created. The files are stored according to their uploaded date. For example, if a file named *book.jpg* is uploaded in May' 2011, then it will be stored as *wp-content/uploads/2011/05/book.jpg*. If the checkbox is not checked, the same file is stored as *wp-content/uploads/book.jpg*

7.4.6 Privacy Settings

Privacy Settings are used for deciding whether we want our blog accessible to search engines or not. It displays two options as shown in Figure 7.37.

- **I would like my site to be visible to everyone, including search engines (like Google, Bing, Technorati) and archivers**—Selecting this option makes our blog visible to everybody including search engines.

- **I would like to block search engines, but allow normal visitors**—Selecting this option hides our blog from search engines and allow human visitors to access our blog. This option also prevents us from pinging linked blogs as well as update services while writing a post. *The Update Services* section of *Writing Settings* becomes invisible and is replaced by the message, *WordPress is not notifying any Update Services because of your site's privacy settings*.

These privacy options apply only to search engine crawlers and other machines. They do not prevent human visitors from seeing our site. To make the whole WordPress site private, we need to install a plugin. There are several plugins that help in making our blog private, few names are, *Private Files, BuddyPress Private Community, Private BuddyPress*, etc.

Privacy Settings

Site Visibility
⦿ I would like my site to be visible to everyone, including search engines (like Google, Bing, Technorati) and archivers
◯ I would like to block search engines, but allow normal visitors

[Save Changes]

Figure 7.37 Privacy Settings Page

7.4.7 Permalink Settings

All our blog contents, posts, pages, categories, archives, etc are accessed through unique URLs. These unique URLs are known as permalinks. Here, perma refers to permanent as URLs of these content should never change. The default permalinks generated by WordPress are not search engine friendly. To generate permalinks, WordPress uses web URL that uses question mark followed by an ID number of the respective posts, pages, categories etc. For example, a default permalink of a post might appear like this:

```
http://example.com.com/?p=100/
```

where p stands for post, and 100 is the ID assigned to the individual post.

In order to allow the search engine spiders to locate our post, it is better to make the permalinks more readable, like, `http://example.com/2010/12/15/working-with-forms/`

where `working-with-forms` is the post slug. To make the search engine friendly permalinks, we open the *Permalink Settings* page by selecting the *Settings->Permalinks* option from the main navigation menu. The Permalink Settings Page appears as shown in Figure 7.38.

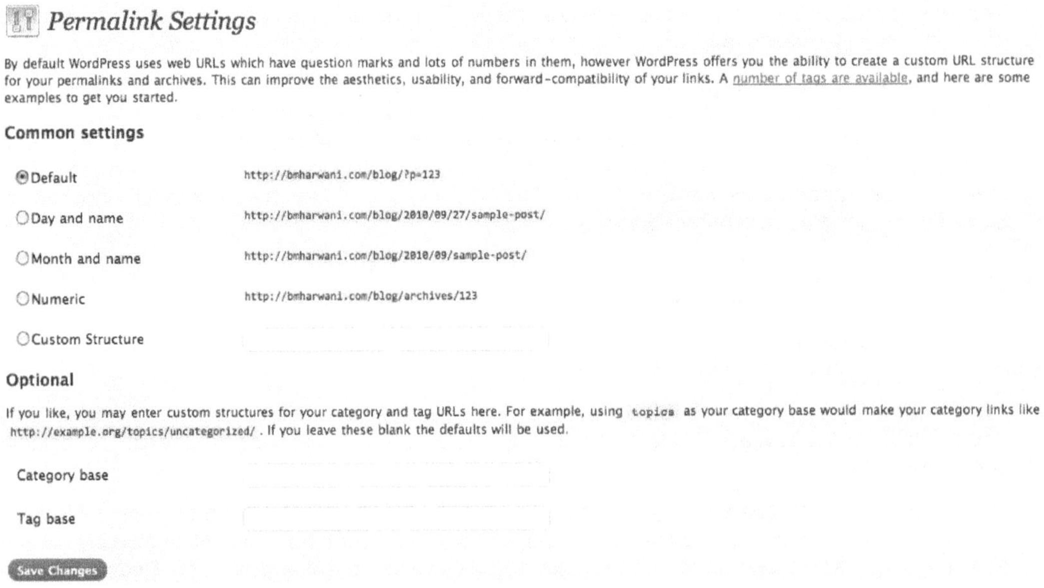

Permalink Settings

By default WordPress uses web URLs which have question marks and lots of numbers in them, however WordPress offers you the ability to create a custom URL structure for your permalinks and archives. This can improve the aesthetics, usability, and forward-compatibility of your links. A number of tags are available, and here are some examples to get you started.

Common settings

⦿ Default   http://bmharwani.com/blog/?p=123

◯ Day and name   http://bmharwani.com/blog/2010/09/27/sample-post/

◯ Month and name   http://bmharwani.com/blog/2010/09/sample-post/

◯ Numeric   http://bmharwani.com/blog/archives/123

◯ Custom Structure

Optional

If you like, you may enter custom structures for your category and tag URLs here. For example, using topics as your category base would make your category links like http://example.org/topics/uncategorized/ . If you leave these blank the defaults will be used.

Category base

Tag base

[Save Changes]

Figure 7.38 Permalink Settings Page

Common Settings

It displays a list of common settings of permalinks to choose from:

- **Default**—In this setting, the permalink displays the ID number that is automatically assigned to each content. As described earlier, the permalink in this setting is not search engine friendly.

Example: `http://example.com/?p=100`.

- **Day and Name**—In this setting, the permalink includes the year, month, day, and post slug.
  Example: `http://example.com/2010/12/15/working-with-forms/`

  where we assume that `working-with-forms` is the post slug.

- **Month and Name**—In this setting, the permalink includes the year, month and post slug.

  Example: `http://example.com/2010/12/working-with-forms/`

- **Numeric**—In this setting, the permalink displays the unique numerical value assigned to the content.

  Example: `http://example.com/archives/100`.

- **Custom Structure**—We can make permalinks to show the information that we want and in desired format. Like, besides the post slug, year etc., we can make permalink to show category name, author name and tags also. To define the custom structure for the permalink, we use a string of structure tags. While defining custom structure, we have to use slashes before tags, between tags, and at the end of the string of tags. A brief description of the structure tags that we can use for defining custom structure is shown in Table 7.3.

Table 7.3 Brief description of Structure Tags

Structure Tags	Output
%year%	Displays year in 4 digits. Example, 2010
%monthnum%	Displays month in 2 digits. Example, 01
%day%	Displays day in 2 digits. Example, 01
%hour%	Displays hour of the day in 2 digits. Example, 13
%minute%	Displays minute in 2 digits . Example, 05
%second%	Displays second in 2 digits . Example, 05
%postname%	Displays the post name, i.e., title. Post names are converted into lowercase and separated by hyphens
%post_id%	Displays the unique numerical ID of the post. Example, 100
%category%	Displays the category name. List post names, they are also converted into lower case and separated by hyphens. Example, smartphone-articles
%author%	Displays name of the post author. Example, bmharwani
%tag%	Displays the tag name. Example, iphone-web-application

Using the information of structure tags displayed above, the custom structure to display year, month, day, category and post slug in the permalinks is given as follows:

`/%year%/%monthnum%/%day%/%category%/%postname%/`

On entering the above string of structure tags in the *Custom Structure* box, the permalink for the post titled *Working with Forms* assigned to the *Smartphone Articles* category and published on 15th Dec, 2010 appears as shown below:

`http://example.com/2010/12/15/smartphone-articles/working-with-forms/`

[147]

> Note: In order to optimize our site for search engine results, it is advisable to choose either of the two common settings: *Day and Name* or *Month and Name*.

Optional

This section is for entering custom bases for the category and tag URLs. By default, the category URL contains the base as *category* and the tag URL contains the base as *tag*. For example, the category URL of post category, *Smartphone Articles* of our blog appear **as**:

http://example.com/category/smartphone-articles/.

Similarly, the tag URL of the tag, *Forms* appears as:

http://example.com/tag/forms/.

We can see in above examples that the default base of categories and tags is *category* and *tag*, respectively. In order to change the default base, we are provided with two options as follows:

- **Category base**—To change the default base of category URL that is *category* by default, we enter the desired text in the *Category base* box. For example, to change the category base to say mobiles, we enter *mobiles* in the *Category base* box. Consequently, the URL of the *Smartphone Article* category becomes:

  http://example.com/mobiles/smartphone-articles/

- **Tag base**—To change the default base of tag URL, which is *tag* by default, we enter the desired text in the *Tag base* box. For example, to change the tag base to say *keywords*, we enter the *keywords* in the *Tag base* box. The URL of tag, *Forms* becomes:

  http://example.com/keyword/forms/

After choosing the desired structure for the permalinks, we save the structure by selecting the *Save Changes* button found at the bottom. We get a message, *Permalink structure updated* if the permalink settings are saved.

> Note: The .htaccess file must be writeable for saving the Permalinks structure.

If *.htaccess* is not writeable, we will be asked to manually update it every time we make changes in the *Permalink Settings* page. On the basis of permalink structure chosen or defined by us, we are provided a list of *mod_rewrite* rules that we have to manually add to our *.htaccess* file.

7.5 Summary

In this chapter, we have seen different options of *Tools* and *Settings* menu. We learned to grab web pages from other sites and publish them on our blog, import contents from other blog to ours, export our blog contents, allow visitors to create account in our blog and set date and time format. We also learned to submit posts via email and through desktop client. We also learnt to define default sizes of media files, make our blog private or public and generate search engine friendly URLs.

In the next chapter, we will be learning things like translating our blog contents in different languages, sharing our posts with Facebook friends, integrate WordPress blog with Twitter account, take online backup of our blog, generate XML sitemaps and much more.

8

Lots More

In the previous chapters, we learned the utility of different options of Tools and Settings menu. We also learned to grab web pages, import and export contents of the blog, allow visitors to register on our blog, set date and time format, submit posts via email and through desktop client, define default sizes of media files, make our blog private or public and generate search engine friendly URLs.

In this chapter, we will learn the following:

- Translating our blog
- Integrating our blog with Facebook
- Integrating our blog with Twitter
- Taking Online Backup
- Generating XML Sitemaps
- Allowing Visitors to Subscribe
- Displaying advertisement for revenue

Let us start with the first task, i.e., translating our blog's contents.

8.1 Translating our blog

Several plugins are available for translating our blog's contents into different languages. However, here I will be using the *GTS Translation WordPress plugin* by *Steven van Loben Sels*. For details of this plugin please visit http://gts-translation.com.

Some features of this plugin are as follows:

- It offers a free solution for translating blog's contents from English to French, Italian, German and Spanish languages.
- It caches the translated content and hence is SEO optimized and indexed by search engines.
- The content is first translated by a translation server followed by editing done by human translators.
- The plugin provides the flexibility to assign the post editing task to either GTS community of translators or to our own community of translators.
- On installation of GTS Translation plugin, the blog's home page is translated along with the posts that appear on the home page.
- All the new posts are automatically translated into the selected languages.

On installing and activating the plugin successfully, a message is displayed at the top of the *Plugins* page: *GTS is almost ready to translate your blog. Please visit the configuration page to get started.* This message contains link to the configuration page. On selecting the link, we get *a GTS Translation* page that prompts us to first register with GTS before starting translation of the blog content. While registering, we are asked several things such as selecting the languages in which we want to translate our blog, whether to immediately publish the machine translated version of our content or only after it is human edited, whether we want GTS editors to manage our blog content or not, etc. (refer to Figure 8.1). After selecting the desired choices, we select the *Next* button to move further.

Figure 8.1 Selecting languages and other options of the GTS plugin

We then get a *License Agreement* page that we need to accept to proceed further. The next page asks for a confirmation whether the URL of our blog and the language chosen for translating our blog content are correct or not. Here, we can select the *Previous* button to go back and change the information that we entered before. Finally, we select the *Finish* button to complete the registration process. A page displaying Congratulations message for successfully configuring our blog for translation is then displayed.

The page (shown in Figure 8.2) also displays the following:

- Blog Id and API Access Key.

- List of languages in which our blog content can be translated. We can select or deselect the language(s), if desired. We can also choose whether to display machine translated version of our content or not.

- Instructions to activate the GTS Language Selector widget so that visitors can use it from the sidebars for translating the blog contents.

GTS Translation

Congratulations! Your blog has been successfully configured and is ready to start translating.
There are other configuration options here that you can now set...

You haven't activated the *GTS Language Selector* widget in your theme. Users won't be able to dynamically change the language. To activate the widget, navigate to the Widgets Panel and drag the *Gts Language Selector* to one of the available sidebars.

Blog ID	kZKcJ5oVNMeG1kdf

API Access Key

UpJZ2krfy25Ak8XFEjF1TcwQRIs2bryk
iBJQGGotgY0zJT0Y3QUdTKmWY2tUWxZI
QBQETa5BwBUFlZCtJilhjJL9M8ARVE2y
t1kEz1QWCTGmH7helt1VJZNVoDkh2ief

Languages

German (Deutsch) : ☑ Virtual Host:

Spanish (Español) : ☑ Virtual Host:

French (Français) : ☑ Virtual Host:

Italian (Italiano) : ☑ Virtual Host:

Display machine-translated content? ☑

Save Changes

Figure 8.2 GTS Translation page displaying Blog ID, API Access key and other information

We select the *Save Changes* button after making the desired modifications. A new menu, *GTS Settings* appears in the main navigation menu with the options as shown in Figure 8.3.

Figure 8.3 GTS Settings menu

The *Translate Theme* option is used to translate the blog's theme template files and the *Manage Posts* option displays the *Translated Posts* as shown in Figure 8.4. From the *Translated Posts* page, we can remove translations of posts that we do not want to be displayed on our blog. The page also displays a link to edit our translated posts.

Translated Posts

Here, you can remove translations of posts that you don't want to be displayed in your blog.

To edit your posts, please go to the GTS Website.

Change Language : French ⬍

Post ID	Post Title	Translated Title	Last Modified	Remove
680	Home	Maison	2010-12-04 17:57:10	Remove
365	Contact Us	Contactez-nous	2010-12-04 17:57:08	Remove
2	About	Au sujet de	2010-12-04 17:57:07	Remove

Figure 8.4 Translated Posts Page

To display the GTS translator in our blog's sidebars, we have to activate the *GTS Language Selector* widget. So, let us open the *Widgets* page by selecting the *Appearance->Widgets* option from the main navigation menu. In the *Widgets* page, we will see one extra widget, *Gts Language Selector* in the *Available Widgets* list. We select this widget and drag it to either sidebar. We can find that in our blog's sidebars, a drop down menu appears titled, *Also available in:* (refer to Figure 8.5(a)). On selecting the drop down menu, we get the language options, French, German, Italian and Spanish (refer to Figure 8.5(b)) to translate our blog contents.

(a)   (b)

Figure 8.5 (a) GTS drop down menu in sidebars (b) Language options in drop down menu

After understanding the technique of translating our blog contents, let us now see how we can integrate our blog's contents with the Facebook.

Facebook is a social networking website owned by Facebook Inc., CA. It is a site where people gather, connect with friends, expand personal network, share feelings, send messages and much more. It also allows developers to contribute applications that interact with the Facebook features.

8.2 Integrating with Facebook

We can make our WordPress blog posts visible in Facebook where visitors can see and respond through writing comments. The plugin, I am going to use for this purpose is *WPBook* by *John Eckman*. For more information about this plugin visit the site, `http://wpbook.net`.

Some features of this plugin are as follows:

- *WPBook* adds our blog as a Facebook application, i.e., Facebook users see our posts in a Facebook look-and-feel environment and write comments with their Facebook identity.

- It allows the comments to be shared by either user, the blog users as well as by Facebook users.

- It automatically posts notification to our wall when a new post is published.

- It import comments made on our wall and displays in our blog as comments.

On installing and activating the plugin a new menu option, *WPBook* is automatically added to the *Settings* menu. On selecting the *WPBook* option from the *Settings* menu, we get the *WPBook Setup* page asking us to register for an API key at Facebook in order to use the WPBook application as shown in Figure 8.6.

WPBook Setup

Please complete all necessary fields

This plugin allows you to embed your blog into the Facebook canvas, allows Facebook users to comment on or share your blog posts, cross-posts your blog posts to the wall of your profile, a fan page, an application profile page, or a group page, and enables users (yourself and other users) to add a tab for your posts to their profile. It also imports comments made against wall posts which originated in WordPress.

Detailed instructions

Required Options:

To use this app, you must register for an API key at Facebook. Follow the link and click "set up a new application." After you've obtained the necessary info, fill in both your application's API and Secret keys as well as your application's url.

Note: Your "Canvas Callback URL" setting in Facebook should be: http://bmharwani.com/blog

Facebook API Key:

Facebook Secret:

Facebook Canvas Page URL, **NOT** INCLUDING "http://apps.facebook.com/"

Stream Publishing Options:

Once your Facebook application is established, return and enter data below.

☐ Publish new posts to YOUR Facebook Wall Profile ID: [?]

☐ Publish new posts to the Wall of this Fan Page, Application Profile Page, or Group: PageID: [?]

Infinite Session Key:

(This key is used for posting to your personal wall, and retrieving comments from your personal wall. If you are not importing comments from a personal wall, it is not necessary. If you are importing comments from a personal wall, and no Infinite Session Key is set, visit the check permissions link above)

☐ Use external permalinks on Walls [?]

☐ Enable WPBook to create a debug file [?]   ☐ Show errors posting to Facebook Stream [?]

Attribution line: [?]
Predefined Strings (you can use these in your attribution line): %author%, %blogname%.

☐ Import comments from Facebook Walls [?]   ☐ Automatically approve imported Wall comments [?]

For how many days should WPBook look for comments on Facebook Walls?:

What email address should WPBook associate with imported comments?

Customize Facebook Application View:

These options will allow you to customize the behavior and display of blog posts in the Facebook application view.

Commenting Options:

☐ Allow comments inside Facebook [?]

Socialize Options:

☐ Show Invite Friends Link [?]   ☐ Enable Add to Profile Button (for Tab): [?]

☐ Enable "Share This Post" (within Facebook) [?]   ☐ Enable "View post at external site" link [?]

Page Options:

☐ Enable pages [?]

General Options:

☐ Include post date with title (you can customize the date format by using the advanced options) [?]

☐ Give WPBook Credit (in Facebook) [?]   ☐ Show a list of recent post below content [?]

☐ Show Advanced Options [?]

(Save)

Figure 8.6 WPBook Setup page

Assuming we are already signed in the Facebook, when we select the *Facebook* link from the *WPBook Setup* page, we get a page titled *Request for Permission*. This page asks for permission to access basic information such as name, profile picture, gender, list of friends, etc. We select the *Allow* button to move further. From the next page, we select the *Set Up new Application* button to create a new application. We are then prompted to specify the application name. Let us enter the application name as http://bmharwani.com/blog. Select the *Agree* option to declare that we agree to the Facebook Terms followed by selecting the *Create Application* button. The application is thus created and we get a link that we need to select to enter some basic information of the application, i.e., of our WordPress blog (refer to Figure 8.7).

Figure 8.7 Page to enter basic information of the application

In the page, we can enter/edit the application name, description, logo and icon. Also, we can specify the language of the blog, email address or URL of the Support, URL to privacy policy and terms of service. We can also add more developers to our application. After entering the desired information, we select the *Save Changes* button to save the changes.

Note: Facebook automatically assigns an *Application ID, API Key* and *Application Secret* key to our application.

On selecting the *Save Changes* button, we get a page displaying a message: *Changes saved*. Note that your changes may take several minutes to propagate to all servers. The page also informs the directory status as *Directory Status: Not Submitted* and displays a *Submit* link to submit the application to the application directory. On selecting the *Submit* link, we get a page for entering information such as Application Name, Contact, Application Description, Logo, etc (refer to Figure 8.8). The entered information is then saved by selecting the *Save* button.

Figure 8.8 Page to submit application to the application directory

We can now find that our WordPress blog posts appear in Facebook at the following URL, `http://apps.facebook.com/bmharwani`. The posts appear in the Facebook look-and-feel environment as shown in Figure 8.9. The links at the top, namely, Pages, About, Contact Us, Home and Posts display the respective information when clicked. Now the visitors and friends can view our blog and write comments on them through Facebook.

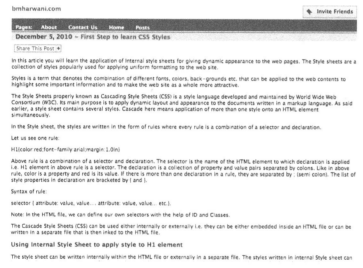

Figure 8.9 Blog contents visible in Facebook

Now onwards, whenever we publish a new post, using the *Add New Post* page, we can find one extra tab, *WPBook* (refer to Figure 8.10) asking whether we want to publish the post on Facebook Wall or not.

Figure 8.10 WPBook tab added to the Add New Post page

After Facebook, let us see how to integrate our blog with Twitter.

Twitter is a social networking website, owned and operated by Twitter Inc. that allows its users to send and read other user's messages, known as tweets.

8.3 Integrating with Twitter

Suppose I want to integrate my WordPress blog with Twitter or in other words I wish to tweet from my WordPress blog. I also want that my tweets on Twitter.com should appear as posts in my WordPress blog. For this purpose, I have chosen the *Twitter Tools* plugin by *Crowd Favorite*. You can have more information about this plugin from its site, http://crowdfavorite.com/wordpress/plugins/twitter-tools. On installing and activating this plugin, a message appears at the top of the *Plugins* page: *Please update your Twitter Tools settings* with a link to set the Twitter Tools options. Also in the *Settings* menu, one menu option is automatically added, *Twitter Tools*. We can choose either way to set the *Twitter Tools* options. The *Twitter Tools Options* page appears as shown in Figure 8.11. The page asks us to register our blog as an application on Twitter.com. The page also guides us about the options that we need to select in the registration page.

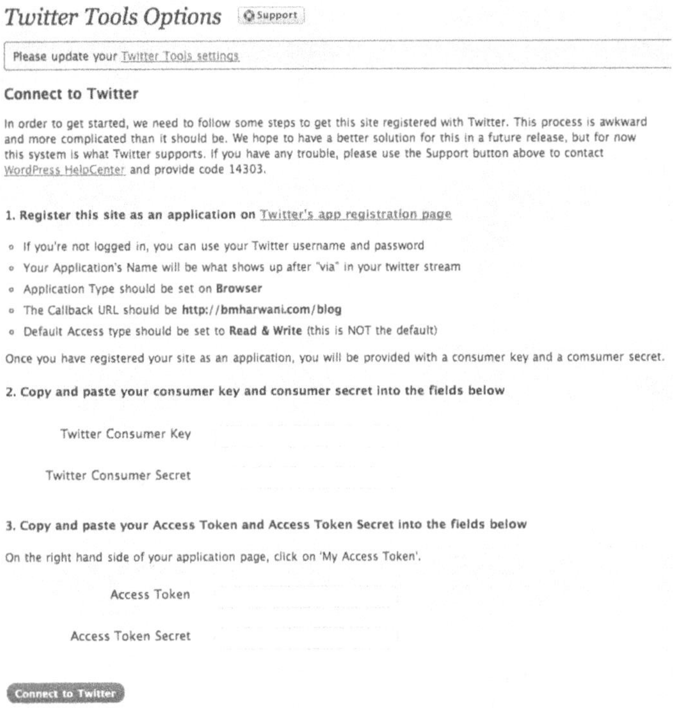

Twitter Tools Options   🔘 Support

Please update your Twitter Tools settings

Connect to Twitter

In order to get started, we need to follow some steps to get this site registered with Twitter. This process is awkward and more complicated than it should be. We hope to have a better solution for this in a future release, but for now this system is what Twitter supports. If you have any trouble, please use the Support button above to contact WordPress HelpCenter and provide code 14303.

1. Register this site as an application on Twitter's app registration page

○ If you're not logged in, you can use your Twitter username and password
○ Your Application's Name will be what shows up after "via" in your twitter stream
○ Application Type should be set on **Browser**
○ The Callback URL should be **http://bmharwani.com/blog**
○ Default Access type should be set to **Read & Write** (this is NOT the default)

Once you have registered your site as an application, you will be provided with a consumer key and a comsumer secret.

2. Copy and paste your consumer key and consumer secret into the fields below

Twitter Consumer Key

Twitter Consumer Secret

3. Copy and paste your Access Token and Access Token Secret into the fields below

On the right hand side of your application page, click on 'My Access Token'.

Access Token

Access Token Secret

[Connect to Twitter]

Figure 8.11 Twitter Tools Options page

The four blank boxes, *Twitter Consumer Key, Twitter Consumer Secret, Access Token* and *Access Token Secret* have to be filled with their respective values auto generated on registering our blog at Twitter.com. These values are required to make our plugin functional. So, let us proceed with the procedure of registering our blog by selecting the link, *Twitter's app registration page*. This link navigates us to the *Twitter Developer's* page where we are prompted to *Sign In* using our Twitter username and password. On entering a valid user name and password, we get a page to register our application. While registering our application, we can take the help of information displayed on the Figure 8.11 meant to guide us. Let us register our blog by entering the information as shown in Figure 8.12.

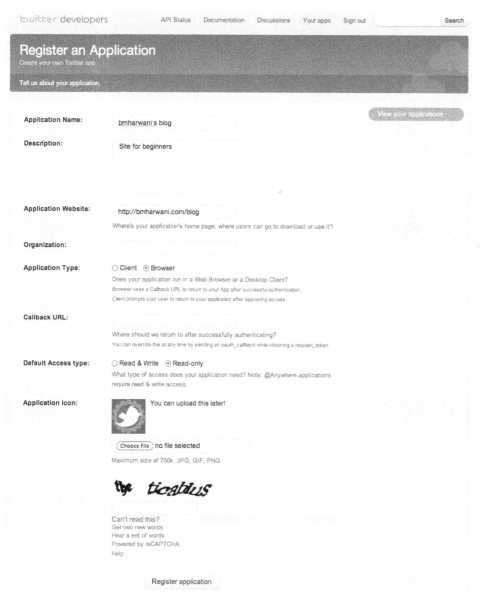

Figure 8.12 Page to register our blog as an application at Twitter.com

On selecting the *Register application* button, we get a page displaying Twitter API Terms of Service. After reading the terms, we need to accept them to use the plugin. We get a page informing that our application has been registered successfully. The page also displays *API key, Consumer Key and Consumer secret key*. The page also displays a button, *My Access Token* that we select to get the *Access Token* and *Access Token Secret* values. We can copy and paste these auto-generated values in the respective *boxes of Twitter Tools Options* page (refer to Figure 8.11). After entering these values, we select the *Connect to Twitter* button to connect our WordPress blog to the Twitter.

The *Twitter Tools Options* displays a message confirming that our blog is connected to the Twitter. The *Twitter Tools Options* page displays a few more options to configure our plugin in detail. These options help us to:

- determine whether to create a tweet when we post in our blog,
- set the Tweet prefix for the new blog posts,
- determine whether to create a blog post from our tweets,
- select the category to assign to the tweet posts,
- define tags for the tweet posts,
- select an author for the tweet posts,
- define the number of tweets to be shown in the sidebars, etc.

After choosing the desired options, we save them by selecting the *Update Twitter Tools Options* button. That is it; the Twitter Tools plugin is configured and fully functional. Now, if I tweet on Twitter.com (refer to Figure 8.13(a)), the tweet will appear as a blog post in our blog as shown in Figure 8.13(b).

Cloud Computing. Wow, I am lik...
5
bmharwani on December 5th, 2010
Cloud Computing. Wow, I am liking it
Smartphone Articles No comments » | Edit
bmharwani Cloud Computing. Wow, I am liking it
2 minutes ago via web

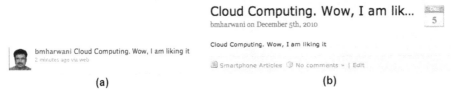

(a) (b)

Figure 8.13 (a) Tweet at Twitter.com (b) Tweet appears in the form of post in the blog

Twitter Tools plugin adds an extra menu option, *Tweet* in *Posts* menu that can be used to create tweets when we post in our blog. On selecting the *Tweet* option from the *Posts* menu we get a *Write Tweet* page (Figure 8.14(a)) where we can write the message. The message not only appears as a blog post on our blog but also appears as a tweet on Twitter.com (Figure 8.14(b)).

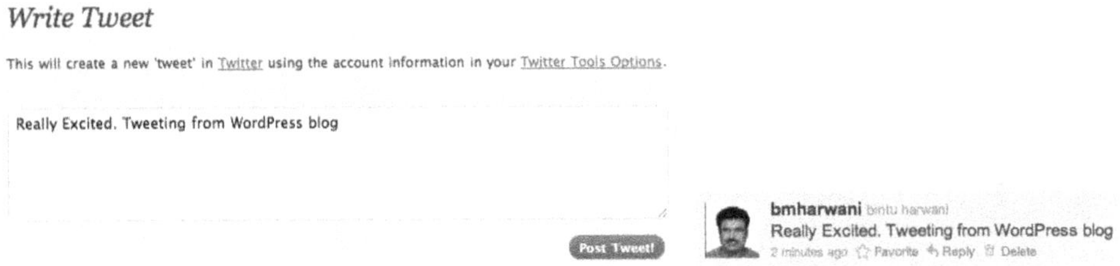
Write Tweet
This will create a new 'tweet' in Twitter using the account information in your Twitter Tools Options.
Really Excited. Tweeting from WordPress blog
Post Tweet!
bmharwani bintu harwani
Really Excited. Tweeting from WordPress blog
2 minutes ago Favorite Reply Delete

(a) (b)

Figure 8.14 (a) Writing Tweet in our blog (b) Tweet written in the blog appears in Twitter.com

To display our latest tweets and to tweet from our sidebars, we can make use of the *Twitter Tools* widget that is automatically added to the *Widgets* page on successful installation of the *Twitter Tools* plugin. So, let us open the *Widgets* page by selecting the *Appearance->Widgets* option from the main navigation menu and drag the *Twitter Tools* widget from the *Available Widgets* list and drop it on either of the sidebars. Let us set the title of the widget to *My Tweets* (Figure 8.15(a)) and select the *Save* button to save the widget. In our blog, we find that our latest tweets appear along with a textbox allowing us to tweet from our blog's sidebars as shown in Figure 8.15(b).

Note: The textbox to tweet appears in the sidebars only when the administrator is logged in.

Figure 8.15 (a) Options of Twitter Tools Widget (b) Latest tweets and textbox to tweet in the sidebars

Now, whenever we publish a new post, in the *Add New Post* page, we can find one extra tab, *Twitter Tools* (Figure 8.16) asking whether we want to send the post to Twitter or not.

Figure 8.16 Twitter Tools tab added to Add New Post page

Let us now see how to save our WordPress blog from disasters.

8.4 Taking Online Backup

It is very important to keep taking backup of our blog contents if we do not want to loose them. For any reason, our blog may be corrupted resulting in loosing all our contents. A blog consists of the following:

- WordPress Core Installation
- Plugins
- Themes
- Posts, comments and the links
- Media Files
- PHP scripts, JavaScript code, and other code files
- Pages

Out of the above, the posts, comments and links are stored in the WordPress database. Again, if we loose WordPress database, we loose all the posts, comments and links of our blog. Therefore, it is better to take backup of everything listed above, i.e., WordPress database as well as other files.

For taking backup of my blog, I am going to use the *Online Backup for WordPress* plugin by *Jason Woods*. You can have more information about the plugin from its site, `http://www.backup-technology.com/2300/online-backup-for-wordpress`.

Few features of the plugin are as follows:

- Offers three backup options
- It provides a smart scheduling option

- Once registered, 50 MB of space on secure servers is offered to an account

- Applies compression and encryption to backed up files

- Emails the backup files

- Provides options like demand backup and locked backup

On successful installation and activation of the plugin, we find three links below the plugin name in the *Plugins Management page*, namely, *Deactivate, Edit* and *View Status*. On selecting the *View Status* link, we get a page that displays information such as when was the previous backup taken, whether backup is scheduled or not, whether compression is enabled or disabled and whether online backup is enabled or not. A few buttons such as *Change Settings, Change Schedule, Decrypt a Backup* and *Refresh* also appear (refer to Figure 8.17) that can be used to configure the backup.

Figure 8.17 Status of Online Backup for WordPress plugin

At this stage we are ready to take backup of our blog manually. While taking backup manually, we need to specify backup targets. We can send the backup files to a specific email address as an attachment or we can download it to our computer or can even send it to the online backup vault. To enable online backup and to save the backup files in the online backup vault, we need to register at the plugin's site, http://www.backup-technology.com/2300/online-backup-for-wordpress. While registering at the plugin's site, we are asked to specify username, password, the blog's URL and the administrator's email address. An activation link is sent to the specified email address for validation. On successful validation of email address, our account is created and we can use it for online backup.

However, before we begin with online backup, we need to set a few things like selecting the *Change Settings* button (refer to Figure 8.17) to open the *Settings* page. The *Settings* page displays the list of tables that are always backed up and the ones that are excluded from backup as shown in Figure 8.18. We can also specify a temporary directory on our server to store the backup file. For online backup, we have to enter the username and password of the account that we created on the plugin's site. The *Settings* page also displays the *Encryption* drop down menu allowing us to encrypt the backup files. We can encrypt our backup file using any of these methods, *DES, AES128, AES192* and *AES256*. After performing the desired settings we save them by selecting the *Save Settings* button.

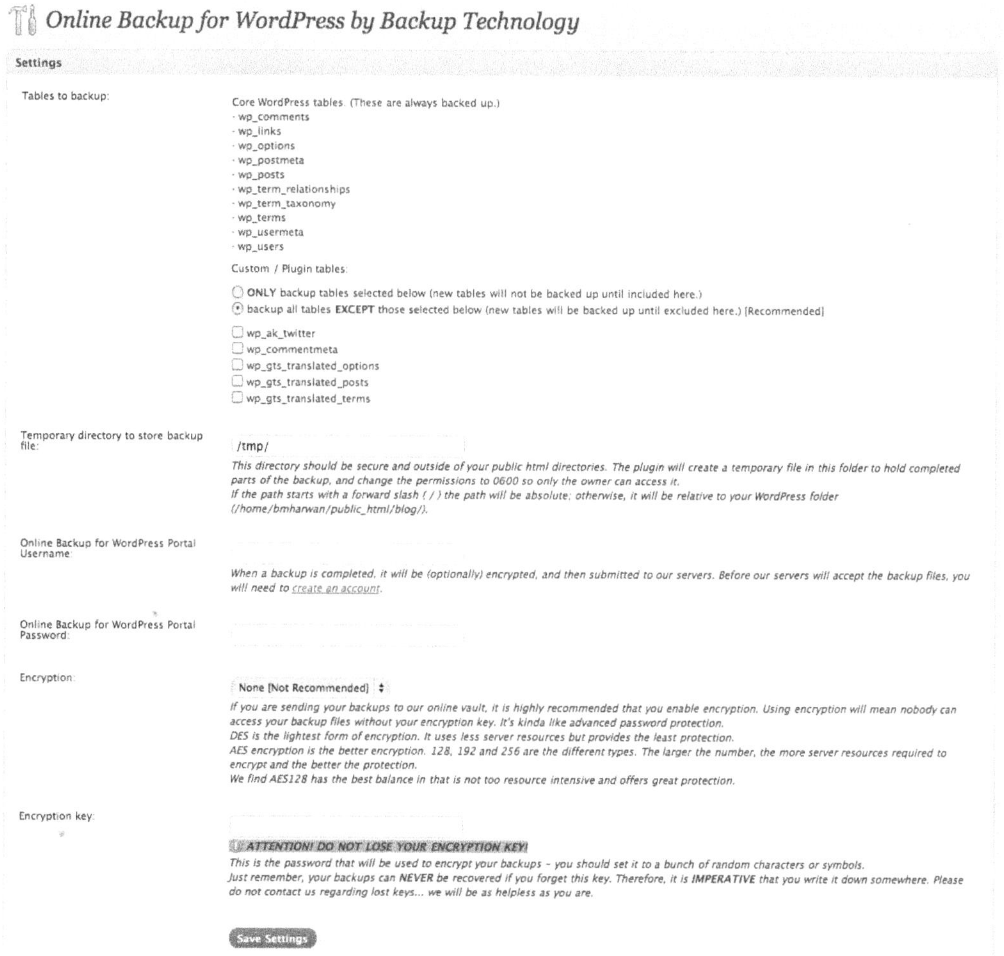

Settings

Tables to backup:	Core WordPress tables. (These are always backed up.) · wp_comments · wp_links · wp_options · wp_postmeta · wp_posts · wp_term_relationships · wp_term_taxonomy · wp_terms · wp_usermeta · wp_users Custom / Plugin tables: ○ **ONLY** backup tables selected below (new tables will not be backed up until included here.) ● backup all tables **EXCEPT** those selected below (new tables will be backed up until excluded here.) [Recommended] ☐ wp_ak_twitter ☐ wp_commentmeta ☐ wp_gts_translated_options ☐ wp_gts_translated_posts ☐ wp_gts_translated_terms
Temporary directory to store backup file:	/tmp/ *This directory should be secure and outside of your public html directories. The plugin will create a temporary file in this folder to hold completed parts of the backup, and change the permissions to 0600 so only the owner can access it.* *If the path starts with a forward slash (/) the path will be absolute; otherwise, it will be relative to your WordPress folder (/home/bmharwan/public_html/blog/).*
Online Backup for WordPress Portal Username:	*When a backup is completed, it will be (optionally) encrypted, and then submitted to our servers. Before our servers will accept the backup files, you will need to create an account.*
Online Backup for WordPress Portal Password:	
Encryption:	None [Not Recommended] ↕ *If you are sending your backups to our online vault, it is highly recommended that you enable encryption. Using encryption will mean nobody can access your backup files without your encryption key. It's kinda like advanced password protection.* *DES is the lightest form of encryption. It uses less server resources but provides the least protection.* *AES encryption is the better encryption. 128, 192 and 256 are the different types. The larger the number, the more server resources required to encrypt and the better the protection.* *We find AES128 has the best balance in that is not too resource intensive and offers great protection.*
Encryption key:	**ATTENTION! DO NOT LOSE YOUR ENCRYPTION KEY!** *This is the password that will be used to encrypt your backups – you should set it to a bunch of random characters or symbols.* *Just remember, your backups can NEVER be recovered if you forget this key. Therefore, it is IMPERATIVE that you write it down somewhere. Please do not contact us regarding lost keys... we will be as helpless as you are.*

Save Settings

Figure 8.18 Settings page of Online Backup for WordPress plugin

We can also set the schedule for automatic online backup by selecting the *Change Schedule* button from the status page (refer to Figure 8.17). Through the *Schedule* page shown in Figure 8.19, we can do several things like:

- Select the schedule for automatic online backup, i.e., whether we want the backup on daily, weekly or on monthly basis.

- Select a weekday for the backup

- Specify hour and minute for taking backup

- Specify email address to send the scheduled backups

- Decide whether we want to send the backup to the online vault or not

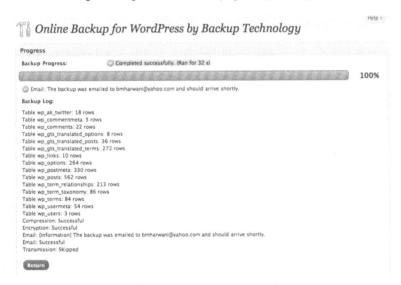

Figure 8.19 Schedule page of Online Backup for WordPress plugin

After setting the schedule, we implement it by selecting the *Apply Schedule* button. When the backup is taken, we get a complete *Backup Log* displaying the list of tables that were backed up as shown in Figure 8.20. The log also displays the status of compression, encryption and email while taking backup, i.e., whether they were executed successfully or not. The log displays encryption and email status only if they were set through Settings and Schedule page, respectively.

Figure 8.20 Backup log displaying status of backup taken

After making our blog safe from disasters by implementing online backup, it is time to think of search engine optimization. So, let us generate an XML sitemap for our blog's contents.

8.5 Generating XML Sitemaps

A sitemap is a complete overview of the posts and pages in our blog. It is used by search engine robots while crawling our blog to find the pages. Here, I will be using *Google XML Sitemaps* plugin by *Arne Brachhold* for generating sitemap of our blog. You can have more information about the plugin from its site, `http://www.arnebrachhold.de/projects/wordpress-plugins/google-xml-sitemaps-generator`.

The Google XML Sitemaps plugin generates a special XML sitemap that helps search engines such as Google, Bing, Yahoo and Ask.com to index our blog better. The sitemap displays the overall structure of our blog and hence makes it easy for crawlers to retrieve it. The plugin supports all kinds of WordPress pages and custom URLs. Whenever a new post is published, all major search engines are automatically informed about it. On installing and activating the plugin, an extra menu option *XML–Sitemap* is automatically added to our *Settings* menu.

On selecting the menu option, *XML-Sitemap* from *Settings* menu, we get a *XML-Sitemap Settings* page that helps in configuring our sitemap file. This page displays several options that can be used to:

- Choose whether to write a normal XML file or gzipped file
- Whether to rebuild sitemap, if any of the blog content is changed
- Whether to notify Google, Bing, Ask.com and Yahoo
- Whether to add sitemap URL to the virtual robots.txt file
- Limit the number of posts in the sitemap
- Include an XSLT stylesheet
- Build the sitemap in a background process
- Specify files or URLs to be included in the sitemap
- Specify how the priority of each post can be calculated
- Location of our sitemap file
- Select the contents to be included in the sitemap. The options are homepage, posts, following pages of multi-pages posts, static pages, categories, archives and tag pages.

The *XML-Sitemap Settings* page also displays a message at the top: *The sitemap wasn't built yet. Click here to build it the first time.* So, let us now go ahead and select the link to generate the sitemap of our blog with default options. On successful generation of the sitemap, we get a page, *XML Sitemap Generator for WordPress* (refer to Figure 8.21) showing the information such as when was sitemap last built, when was zipped format of sitemap last built, which of the search engines (Google, Bing and Ask.com) were notified and how much time it took to notify each of them, etc.

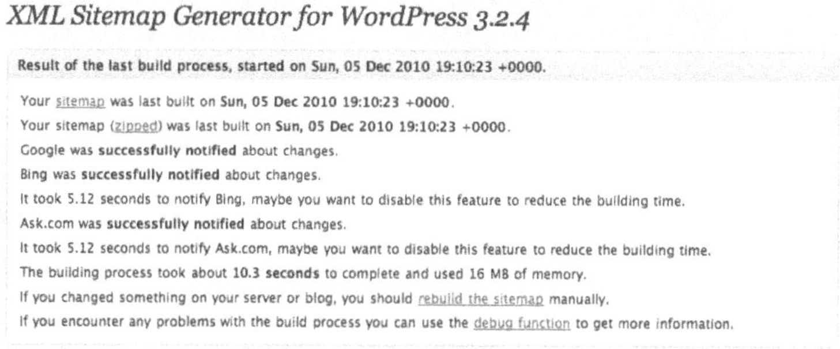

XML Sitemap Generator for WordPress 3.2.4

Result of the last build process, started on Sun, 05 Dec 2010 19:10:23 +0000.

Your sitemap was last built on **Sun, 05 Dec 2010 19:10:23** +0000.
Your sitemap (zipped) was last built on **Sun, 05 Dec 2010 19:10:23** +0000.
Google was **successfully notified** about changes.
Bing was **successfully notified** about changes.
It took 5.12 seconds to notify Bing, maybe you want to disable this feature to reduce the building time.
Ask.com was **successfully notified** about changes.
It took 5.12 seconds to notify Ask.com, maybe you want to disable this feature to reduce the building time.
The building process took about **10.3 seconds** to complete and used 16 MB of memory.
If you changed something on your server or blog, you should rebuild the sitemap manually.
If you encounter any problems with the build process you can use the debug function to get more information.

Figure 8.21 Page showing information about the generated blog's sitemap

Also, we get a message, *Sitemap Notification Received* informing that our sitemap is successfully added to the list of Sitemaps to crawl (refer to Figure 8.22). We will also get a URL that we can use to track the status of our sitemap.

Sitemap Notification Received

Your Sitemap has been successfully added to our list of Sitemaps to crawl. If this is the first time you are notifying Google about this Sitemap, please add it via http://www.google.com/webmasters/tools/ so you can track its status. Please note that we do not add all submitted URLs to our index, and we cannot make any predictions or guarantees about when or if they will appear.

Figure 8.22 Notification informing successful addition of blog's sitemap to the list of Sitemaps

We can view the sitemap by pointing the browser at `http://bmharwani.com/blog/sitemap.xml`.

Note: sitemap.xml is added as a suffix to our blog's URL for viewing the sitemap.

The sitemap of our blog looks like as shown in Figure 8.23.

XML Sitemap

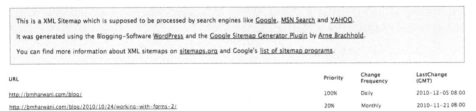

URL	Priority	Change Frequency	LastChange (GMT)
http://bmharwani.com/blog/	100%	Daily	2010-12-05 08:00
http://bmharwani.com/blog/2010/10/24/working-with-forms-2/	20%	Monthly	2010-11-21 08:00

Figure 8.23 XML Sitemap of our blog

By generating the sitemap of our blog, we have certainly improved search engine optimization of our site as all our site contents are now be accessible to the crawlers.

What if any of the visitors likes our blog contents and wish to subscribe? Let us see how to do that.

8.6 Allowing Visitors to Subscribe

To allow visitors of my blog to subscribe, I have used here the *FeedBurner Subscription Widget (English)* plugin by *Technology 4 Lives*. For more information about this plugin, you can visit the site `http://www.tech4lives.com`. The plugin can be used to display a FeedBurner email subscription form on the sidebars of our blog. It can also be customized to display the type of information we want. We can also get to know the number of subscribers to our blog through this plugin.

Note: FeedBurner, owned by Google provides several feed management tools that are available to be used freely.

On installing and activating the plugin, we can find one extra widget, *FeedBurner Subscription* added to our list of *Available Widgets* in *Widgets* page. To display the email subscription form or link to email subscription form in the sidebars, we can either make use of the *FeedBurner Subscription* widget or use the Email Subscription code generated by FeedBurner, as we will soon see. But the first pre-requisite condition to use this plugin is to have FeedBurner ID and FeedBurner User URL, which we can get only on registering at FeedBurner. So, let us see how to register at FeedBurner.

On visiting the FeedBurner's URL, `http://feedburner.google.com`, we get a *Google feedburner* page asking for signing with the user name and password of our Google Account. On entering a valid email address and password, we get *My Feeds* page as shown in Figure 8.24. The *My Feeds* page asks us to enter the URL of our blog feed. The blog's feed URL of the WordPress blog is created by adding /feed suffix to our blog's URL. For example, if my blog's URL is http://bmharwani.com/blog, then the blog feed's URL will be http://bmharwani.com/blog/feed. After entering the blog's feed URL, select the *Next* button to move further.

Figure 8.24 My Feeds page on Google feedburner

We get a Welcome page on verification of our blog's feed address. The page also informs us that the new feed will be activated in our FeedBurner account. The page displays the default *Feed Title* and *Feed Address* that we can edit if desired. Select the *Next* button to move to the next page. On following the instructions that appears in the subsequent pages, we get a page displaying Congratulations message: *'Congrats! Your FeedBurner feed is now live. Want to dress it up a little?'*. The page also displays the *FeedBurner User URL* and other related information.

One last thing that is left to make our plugin functional is to activate *Email Subscriptions* service. For activating Email Subscription service, we select the *Publicize* tab. When we select the *Publicize* tab, on the left-hand side several services are listed. From the list of services displayed, we can select the *Email Subscriptions* service. We get page informing that email subscription form and its HTML code will be provided to us if we activate the service by selecting the *Activate* button provided at the bottom (refer to Figure 8.25).

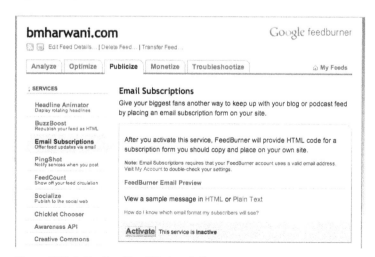

Figure 8.25 Activating Email Subscriptions

On selecting the *Activate* button, we get a page that displays HTML code for:

- Email subscription form where visitor can enter email address to subscribe

- Link which when selected navigates the user to the email subscription form to enter the email address

We can use these codes to display the Email subscription form or Email subscription link in the sidebars through the *Text* widget.

One thing to note is that our newly published posts are not mailed to our subscribers immediately but in between the time interval that is set by us. To set the time interval of the delivery of our posts, we select the *Delivery Options* link under *Email Subscriptions* service. We get a page (refer to Figure 8.26) to select the *time zone* and *time slot window*. After setting *time zone* and *time slot window*, we select the *Save* button to save the delivery options. Now our subscribers get the mails in the selected timeslot of the specified time zone.

Figure 8.26 Setting email delivery schedule for the subscribers

To use the *Text* widget we open the *Widgets* page by selecting the *Appearance->Widgets* option from the main navigation menu. From the *Available Widgets* list, drag the *Text* widget and drop it in either of the sidebars. Paste the code of email subscription form in the box and assign the *Title* as *Subscribe* (refer to Figure 8.27(a)) followed by selecting the *Save* button. On our blog, an email subscription form with the title *Subscribe* appears as shown in Figure 8.27(b). The email subscription form displays a textbox where visitors can enter their email address to subscribe to our blog.

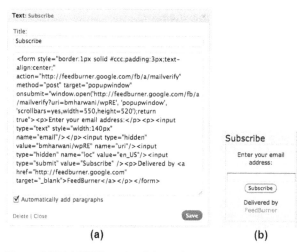

(a)   (b)

Figure 8.27 (a) HTML code of Email Subscription form in Text widget (b) Email Subscription form in the sidebars

If we paste the code of the link to the email subscription form in the *Text* widget (refer to Figure 8.28(a)), instead of email subscription form, a link, *Subscribe to bmharwani.com by Email* appears in the sidebars of our blog (Figure 8.28(b)). On selecting the link, visitors get an email subscription form to enter their email address.

(a)   (b)

Figure 8.28 (a) HTML code of Link to Email Subscription form in Text widget (b) Link to Email Subscription form in the sidebars

When a visitor enters his/her email address in the email subscription form and selects the *Subscribe* button, an email verification process is initiated. A page is displayed informing that our request has been accepted and asks us to open our email and select the provided link to verify the email address. On selecting the link provided in the mail, we get a message, *Email Subscription Confirmed* that means all our newly published posts are automatically mailed to the visitor in the specified time slot. A sample of the mail received by the subscriber displaying latest published post is as shown in Figure 8.29.

Figure 8.29 Email sent to the subscriber showing the latest post(s)

Note: The email to the subscribers also contains a link to unsubscribe, if desired.

Not only blogs are a great means to update our visitors and developing relations with them but also quite helpful in generating revenues. How? Let us see.

8.7 Displaying ads for revenue

We can generate revenue from our blog by displaying advertisement and promoting affiliate programs. Selling advertising is one of the popular methods of generating revenues. We can generate revenue by displaying Google AdSense or by promoting products as an Amazon associate. For displaying Google AdSense, we have to signup for an AdSense account. Google reviews our application and if it is approved, we can log into the AdSense home page.

We can also earn money through affiliate programs in Amazon Associates. Again, we have to first sign up to be an Amazon associate. After our application is approved, we can place links to different products on Amazon in our blog. The link contains a unique ID assigned to us by Amazon and when any of our referrals makes a purchase, we get some percentage of the sale. We can display the Amazon products in the form of banners at the top, mid or bottom of our blog posts. We can also display products on the sidebars.

On logging into the Amazon Associate's member's area, we get several options to choose from. Like, we are presented with links, *Links & Banners, Widgets, Site Strips*, etc. and we can choose the one that we want to display on our blog. On selecting a link, say *Links & Banners*, we are asked whether we want to link to a specific product or link to a banner that promotes the products belonging to an Amazon category. On choosing an option, say, banner we get a list of product categories to choose from. For example, on selecting a category say *Kindle*, we are provided HTML codes for banners of different sizes as shown in Figure 8.30.

Figure 8.30 HTML code for the banner of the selected category

To display advertisements in the sidebars, we can directly copy the generated HTML code and paste it in a Text widget. To display, the advertisement at any location in our blog, using a plugin is the best option. To display an advertisement, I am going to use a plugin, *Ad Injection* by *reviewmylife*. For more information on this plugin, you can visit the site, http://www.reviewmylife.co.uk/blog/2010/12/06/ad-injection-plugin-wordpress/

Few of the features of this plugin are as follows:

- It can inject any kind of advertisement such as Google AdSense, Amazon Associates, ClickBank, etc.

- Advertisements can be injected into existing posts without modifying the posts.

- The number of advertisements can be set on the basis of the length of the post.

- We can restrict the advertisements to be displayed only on the posts that are defined numb roof days old.

- We can block IP addresses of the people whom we do not want to be able to see our ads

- We can position (left, right, center, etc.) our advertisement as per our desire.

On installing and activating our plugin, a message is displayed on the Plugins page at the top: *Ad Injection needs configuring. Go to the settings page to configure and enable your ads.* We can select the link provided in the message to access the *Ad Injection's Settings* page. We can also access the plugin's settings page by selecting the menu option, *Ad Injection* that is automatically added to the *Settings* menu on successful installation of the plugin.

The *Ad Injection's Settings* page displays respective boxes for pasting the codes provided by advertisers for injecting advertisements in our blog. We can use these options to inject the advertisements wherever we want, in the mid of the posts, at the top of the post, bottom, on the sides. We can also configure the number of ads in a post, exclude certain posts from ads, display ads on selected types of posts, and so on.

On pasting the HTML code that is provided by the advertiser in the *Optional top advert* box with the options set as shown in Figure 8.31(a). The advertisement appears at the top of the post as appears in Figure 8.31(b).

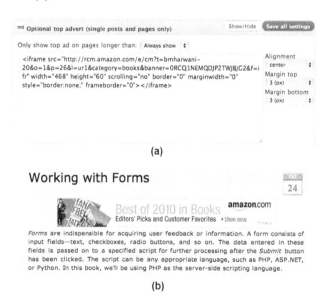

(a)

(b)

Figure 8.31 (a) HTML code for displaying banner at the top of the posts (b) Banner displayed at the top of the post

Similarly, on pasting the code in *Randomly Injected ad* code box with the options set as shown in Figure 8.32(a), the advertisement may appear in the mid of our post as shown in Figure 8.32(b).

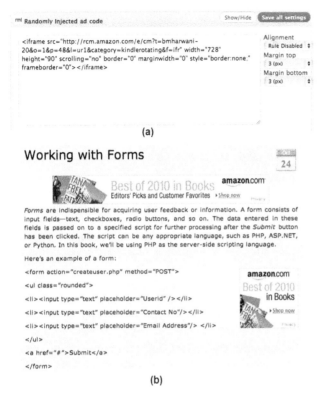

(a)

(b)

Figure 8.32 (a) HTML code for displaying banner in the mid of the posts (b) Banner displayed at the top and mid of the post

Hence, we can use Ad Injection for displaying ads at the desired places with the desired contents of our blog.

8.8 Summary

In this chapter, we learned to do several things such as translating our blog, integrating our blog with Facebook and Twitter, taking Online Backup, generating XML Sitemaps, allowing visitors to subscribe to our blog and generating revenue by displaying ads on our blog.

In this book, I have tried my best to keep things easy to understand. I hope you would agree. You now have all the necessary information for building and maintaining your own blog.

Have fun creating your blog, and thanks for reading!

Index

Symbols

A

M

N

O

P

T

X

Y

www.ingramcontent.com/pod-product-compliance
Lightning Source LLC
Chambersburg PA
CBHW080413060326
40689CB00019B/4225